LOW CARB REVOLUTION

COMFORT EATING FOR GOOD HEALTH

ANNIE BELL

Foreword by Dr Alexander D. Miras MRCP, PhD

LOW CARB REVOLUTION

COMFORT EATING FOR GOOD HEALTH

ANNIE BELL

Foreword by Dr Alexander D. Miras MRCP, PhD

Photography by Dan Jones

Illustrations by Sam Wilson

Kyle Books

Contents

Foreword by Dr Alexander D. Miras MRCP, PhD

Weight loss through caloric restriction has attracted an enormous interest, both from the public and the 'dieting' industry, because of the profound rise in the incidence of obesity in many parts of the globe. Even though dieting works very well in the short term, the longer term results are disappointing, with only a minority actually achieving sustained weight loss. This outcome can be very frustrating for the dieter who wants to improve their health and well-being. Whilst it is often easy for healthcare professionals to blame the individual for lack of willpower, to date calorie restriction has failed to solve the problem of obesity and its associated diseases. Diet 'failure' is almost the natural result of a number of physiological mechanisms resisting fat loss, which is associated with an evolutionary disadvantage. In fact, considering the calorie-dense environment we all live in, our genetics and the hormonal mechanisms that control our body weight, it is very surprising how up to 20% of dieters do manage to maintain their weight loss, and why even more people aren't obese!

A more successful approach to dieting has been to change the macronutrient composition (ie proportion of protein, fat and carbohydrates) of what we eat. The best available evidence so far tells us that weight loss and/or maintenance can most readily be achieved through the consumption of a diet which is high in protein and low in carbohydrates. What is very interesting is that participants in these clinical research trials were allowed to eat as much as they wished, as long as they got the macronutrient balance right. The reasons as to why diets high in protein can be more effective are not fully clear yet, but further research has shown that they are particularly good at reducing hunger and increasing fullness.

I was very interested to find that Annie Bell, the author of this book, came to the same conclusion through real-life experiences and research. These experiences provide much needed support to the sometimes sterile findings of a research trial or experiment. Her approach in this book is very different to the previous literature; she has developed recipes that can be readily introduced into daily cooking and adopted as a completely normal way of eating, rather than an uphill struggle. I enjoyed reading the recipes and endorse this novel and exciting approach to eating. I hope that the readers of the book also find the recipes delicious and satisfying, whilst benefiting from better health and overall well-being.

Dr Alexander D.Miras MRCP, PhD
Clinical Lecturer in Metabolic Medicine, Imperial College, London

A personal odyssey

When I went through a period of appetite loss a couple of years ago, I had no idea it was the beginning of a long journey that would change the way I look at food and how I eat. At a professional level, for every recipe I devise for salad I probably devise at least ten for cakes, and as far as diets are concerned, I am more of a voyeur than a participant. So it has been a journey through uncharted territory.

If I travel back to my childhood, I was never a beanpole. My mother saw to it that I carried enough weight to cope with an emergency, even though that never extended beyond a class epidemic of chickenpox. I think, quite simply, she loved to feed us, and I too am guilty of this with others. I can still recall with some nostalgia the taste of the spoonful of malt extract that was provided as insurance after breakfast during the winter. But as I'm not someone who can eat whatever they want without consequence, I arrived in my late teens with enough 'emergency supplies' to cope not only with my own chickenpox but that of several others as well.

This wasn't a problem. With enough late nights, cigarettes, tangled love affairs and whatever else, it disappeared. But, as I progressed through my thirties, a couple of children and then my forties, there was an incipient weight gain. Or, as a friend once remarked when *Mad Men* mania swept through the high street, 'fashion's made for you this summer'. I think she meant it nicely. Though if I was on the curvy side I was also quite happy with it. I could see enough pluses, and, as someone who has always suffered from emotional appetite loss, I figured there was in any case probably something round the corner that would take care of it. Anything that involved family members and hospitals, and I could guarantee I would be several kilos lighter a few weeks down the line. But, the reality was, that as soon as my appetite returned to normal the weight would start creeping back on again, just as surely as bust follows boom.

Then, however, after one such period of quite severe appetite loss something changed. The only foods I had been able to face for weeks (or months) on end were roast chicken and vegetable soup, and in small quantities; my idea of comfort food at the time. It wasn't until the end of this episode that it occurred to me that I had inadvertently given up starchy carbohydrates, and by this stage I had actually lost my taste for them. My appetite was up and running again, but my natural inclination was to indulge in lots of roasts and fish, and all my favourite vegetables and seasonal fruits. I also realised that a whole host of niggling discomforts had simply disappeared. I felt better, more energised, satisfied after eating but never overfull, and I could eat any amount without feeling that sense of regret that comes with 'I wish I hadn't eaten that'. In short, it felt right and natural.

And so I decided to continue eating this way, to ditch the bread, the potatoes, the pasta and rice that I would once have eaten as an accompaniment and see how I got on. Over two years down the line, as well as still loving this way of eating I continue to be amazed that despite eating heartily – far more than I ever used to and at times more than my husband – my weight hasn't increased by so much as half a kilo. That constancy gives me huge pleasure, and a sense of security that has come as a surprise. And it left me feeling that if it really is that easy, I ought to be passing it on.

Fashionably low in carbs

If I had inadvertently arrived to worship at the altar of Low Carb, there were any number of others who had got there before me. As a means of weight loss it has hardly been out of the news since Dr Robert Atkins launched his book *Dr Atkins' Diet Revolution* in 1972. But for those, like me, who grew up on the receiving end of the government's food pyramid, it still represents a seismic shift in thinking.

The government's proposed ideal diet at the end of the twentieth century had us all stuffed with starchy complex carbohydrates such as pasta, potatoes and bread, the base of a pyramid, with just a little in the way of protein that occupied the tip, and more or less the same amount of dairy, with fruit and veg filling in the middle section. It may have worked for a few, but not many, and in effect supported the carb-heavy popular food culture that exists today, which we now know to be responsible for so much obesity.

Popular food culture could be seen as the pyramid taken to its unhealthiest extreme. Unless you have a very unusual metabolism, there is every chance that you will be setting yourself up for a life of yo-yo diets and 'giving up' foods in order to reduce your weight, so that you can get back to the carbs that form the basis of how you eat – until, that is, you are forced to give them up again. But, with every cycle, you are probably gaining more and more weight (Low Cal v. Low Carb, page 10). So although it might taste good at the time, it's a pretty miserable cycle.

Dr Robert Atkins has since been joined by the South Beach Diet, the Zone Diet and, most famously, the Dukan Diet. Each of these regimes is very specific and scientifically based, and individually may find fans among those seeking to lose weight quickly. But even without the rigour of such a system, simply reducing your level of carbohydrate intake, be it through avoiding pure sugar or starchy foods, appears to be the easiest and most effective means of maintaining your weight at a desirable level. You don't have to be tackling the extremes of obesity to make use of this system.

What happens when we lose weight?

When we talk about appetite we tend to talk in terms of what we 'feel' like eating. And psychology certainly comes into it (The Psychology of Hunger, page 11) but, more importantly, there is a puppet master inside our brains called the hypothalamus that is pulling the strings via a series of hormones and nerves that control our urges and appetite, hence what and how much we eat, and how much energy we then expend, which together adds up to controlling our weight.

The hypothalmus also receives information about our fat stores and calorie intake through hormones produced by fat cells and the gut. For example leptin, or the 'fat' hormone, is produced by fat cells and the more of it, the less hungry you feel. When you lose weight, leptin levels go down and this increases your hunger. Through starving, you also increase the level of ghrelin, the 'hunger' hormone produced in the stomach that is normally suppressed by food when you eat. On the flip side, there are less of the 'satiety' hormones PYY and GLP-1, which are responsible for making us feel full, and therefore you continue to feel hungry. Effectively by starving the body you activate its emergency plan to restore the natural order, which it does by setting aside some fat for a rainy day.

To make matters worse, the hypothalamus which has been activated by your weight loss gets in touch with the sympathetic nervous system which controls your calorie burning and it alerts the rest of your body to reduce the metabolic rate in order to conserve energy, therefore calorie burning goes down.

The combination of these short- and long-term hormonal and nerve reactions to reducing the amount that you eat eventually leads you to start regaining any weight you have lost.

Low cal v. low carb

'Dieting', says Dr Alexander D. Miras, 'is very effective for weight maintenance, but unfortunately only causes weight loss in the short term.' The pattern is, that after an initial period of weight loss, due to the complex hormonal reaction just described, your weight will then plateau, and then it will start to rise again.

'Within 1–2 years the vast majority of people who go on a diet regain the weight they have lost, and some may even end up at a weight higher than one they started with. This is not because we are 'weak' or not-disciplined enough, but because evolution has programmed us to either keep our weight the same or gain weight. This has allowed us to survive through famine and war.'

And this is where the difference in approaches between Low Calorie and Low Carbohydrate comes in. Dr Miras has specialised in treating obesity and diabetes as well as conducting clinical trials for five years, at Imperial College. 'A significant number of patients we see in our clinics are yo-yo dieters', explains Dr Miras, 'and if they are on a low or very Low Calorie diet I can almost guarantee that the vast majority will regain more weight in the long-term than the amount they have lost.'

Compare that with High Protein Low Carb diets, which trials have shown to be more effective than any other form of dieting in both the short and the long term. If there is any weight regain it is much slower and less than what has been observed in other calorie-reduced diets. In Dr Miras's experience, 'the available data, from studies in which different diets have been compared, tell us that High Protein Low Carb diets offer the best solution to sustainable weight loss and maintenance.'

The magic ingredient

The psychology of hunger

I know from personal experience that if I start off the day eating fruit, and yogurt perhaps, that I will continue to snack throughout the morning until I eat some protein and get that sensation that translates as 'feeling full'. It is a very attractive 'full'; whereas starchy carbohydrates can leave you feeling weary and bloated, protein leaves you with a sense of being satisfied in a way that is clean and light. It also leaves you feeling full for longer.

But if it feels like that in practice, scientists still don't completely understand why. As Dr Miras puts it, 'certain diets can fool the hypothalamus to reduce hunger while losing weight at the same time, which is where High Protein comes in. We don't understand the mechanism of protein on hunger, but the protein itself reduces hunger and increases fullness more than fat or carbohydrate. With less carbohydrate in the system, the liver produces more ketone bodies, and there is some evidence that these can also fool the hypothalamus, making you less hungry and more full. As a result weight loss and its maintenance are easier.'

Perhaps one of the most interesting observations concerns bariatric (weight-loss) surgery. 'With a gastric bypass, we don't completely understand why, but patients automatically follow a High Protein Low Carbohydrate diet post-surgery. This has very little to do with advice we give them before this particular type of surgery, which is also the most effective, it is almost as if it is the patients' hormones and changed anatomy that are now guiding their food choices. This suggests to me that there must be an advantage in consuming diets high in protein and low in carbohydrates.'

So there is strong evidence to suggest, that if you are seeking to lose weight and to keep it off, the best way to achieve this is through restricting your carbohydrate intake and eating more protein.

If I say the word 'diet' and ask you to write down the first five things that come into your mind, then it will probably run something along the lines of 'denial', 'small portions', 'hunger', 'grim food', 'horrible'. I would agree.

Reading about any diet that involves fasting or cutting down, I freeze over simply trying to think through the effect of what it involves. Less food, no food? Giving up? The idea of sitting shivering at my computer, so hungry that I could eat the carpet, fills me with dread.

As sensations go, hunger is one of my least favourite. The yearning for whatever I am being denied overrides what I am doing, to a disproportionate degree until I can think of nothing else. I am left feeling empty and wanting, a little *triste* perhaps, dreaming of sunny climes and unable to concentrate.

I am not alone in needing to feel full and well-fed in order to function properly. We have an inbuilt reward mechanism that acts like a small voice when we have denied ourselves food that tells us we deserve a treat. This kicks in with Low Calorie dieting with a vengeance, making it almost impossible to maintain in the long term. However, with a diet that is high in protein but low in carbohydrates, because you are eating normal quantities of food – and potentially delicious food – that mechanism is kept at bay. Or, as Dr Miras puts it, 'High Protein Low Carb diets work because they are bearable in the long-term, they offer a normal living diet.'

Low Calorie diets, in contrast, fly in the face of what is natural. We need to be able to eat as much as we want, without being on a guilt trip or trying to rein in our appetite as if it were a bolting horse, by stopping eating before we are satiated. Restrictive diets as such are not a long-term solution, they're a short-term fix. They're unrealistic, a temporary suspension of normal play.

Back in the kitchen

I was fascinated to discover that there were sound scientific reasons for my own experience. But back in the kitchen, as someone whose life revolves around cooking and eating, I found what was on offer was lacking. Nearly all the recipes I encountered for avoiding carbohydrates were 'diet' recipes, austere and unalluring, and a far cry from the comfort food that I have always loved and associated with family occasions.

Whether you have been on the Dukan Diet, the South Beach, the Atkins or simply chose to be careful about your carbohydrate intake, you are more or less left stranded in the desert in terms of a normal way of eating on a sustained basis.

And hence *Low Carb Revolution* was born. I wanted to give all our favourite family dishes, as well as popular café and fast-food fare that is so often carb-heavy, a healthy make-over. Here are chapters like Burger Bar, Chop House, The Carvery, and Mash, Chips or Roast that are a celebration of our traditional comfort foods.

The dishes we grow up with form part of our cultural make-up, carrying with them a whole host of associations. I always derive a sense of comfort and feeling of well-being when I put a Shepherd's Pie on the table or serve up a Sunday roast with all the trimmings. Then there are dishes that I recall my mother cooking as a child and that I have continued to cook for my own family. Life without them would be poorer. And come a Friday or Saturday night, the craving for scampi or steak and chips might set in, in the same way as a Spanish omelette with salad makes the perfect Sunday night supper before sinking into the sofa to watch a seasonal period drama. I see no reason to give up what we love and are familiar with.

The style of these recipes is no different to any others I have devised over the years – they are intentionally hearty, relaxed and rustic, designed to be family-friendly and inclusive of other diners. The idea is that you can add the carbs back in as asides in the way of potatoes, bread, rice or pasta for those that want, and maybe also need them. I don't, for instance, need the same level of sustenance as my six foot two teenager, who might have an early morning rowing session followed by a full day at school and then rugby, travel home and continue working. The aim here is very much a way of eating that can be layered to suit the different needs of your various family members.

And it is real food too, it's not about low-fat sprays and artificial sweeteners. I have simply tried to temper those aspects by using only what is necessary to cook the dish and for it to taste alluring. So there is no gratuitous oil or cream. Is that extra drizzle of oil on the veggies really necessary, or that large dollop of crème fraîche in the centre of the soup bowl? In truth, it probably isn't going to make any difference to how good it is to eat; sometimes we are adding a little luxury with such finishing touches, but ultimately the dish is just as good without.

This is the food that I cook and eat every day, because this is the food that I love. Based on seasonal vegetables with herbs and spices, olive oil and occasionally a little sour cream when called for, and simply grilled and roasted meat and fish. It's food that leaves me feeling satiated but light and clean, and really energised. Consider it a good springboard, whatever else you might want to add in (courtesy of what I do I still get to taste chocolate cake five times a day), it serves as a starting point and foundation.

Carb counting

Snacking

I have never personally counted the number of carbs that I eat. The dishes that follow are naturally low in carbohydrates, so simply by choosing these over starchy carbs and sugar you are radically reducing your intake.

But, for those who are on a diet or regime that does require them to be counted, the respective quantities of both carbs and protein have been calculated by a nutritionist. You will also find values for the total carbohydrate and protein content of the dish, when there are optional extras suggested.

There is, however, a fairly widely accepted figure of 100g carbohydrate per day, below which you should lose weight quite rapidly if that is your goal. In terms of weight maintenance, Dr Christina G. Prechtl (Post-doctoral Researcher and Dietetic Therapist in Obesity, Imperial College London) recommends that you can increase that amount. Equally, you can decrease it if the 100g marker doesn't work for you.

For those who want to explore further the nutrient quality of what they are eating, McCance and Widdowson's *The Composition of Foods* (Royal Society of Chemistry, www.rsc.org), approved by the Food Standards Agency, is the well-regarded authority on the subject, with a comprehensive breakdown of every ingredient.

Bearing in mind the role played by protein, if you are going to snack between meals then it is a good idea to include a little with whatever you are eating.

Dr Prechtl further recommends limiting fruit to two pieces per day (one if you are seeking to lose weight), or even omitting it altogether if you are struggling. That said, the ones to aim for are berries – strawberries, raspberries, blackberries and blueberries, also greengages and plums, guavas, Cantaloupe melon and passionfruit. The ones which are particularly high in carbohydrates and to avoid are bananas, oranges, cherries and grapes.

Kitchen kit and suppliers

Non-stick

Non-stick frying pans and saucepans come into their own when you are trying to reduce the amount of fat you cook with. Meats such as chicken (with its skin), lamb and pork all have enough fat within them to forego adding any extra to the pan, providing there is no chance of them sticking. Salmon too, can be dry-fried.

But, such is the delicacy of non-stick pans that even the most expensive will wear out within a year of regular use. So, it is wise to buy carefully. The good news, however, is the increasing prevalence of different types of non-stick, and improvements in more traditional coatings too. So here are a few recommendations:

CERAMIC NON-STICK

I am a huge fan of these ceramic Thermolon-coated non-stick pans that are PTFE-free. Unlike other non-stick pans, which are rarely good for anything once the coating has worn out, these enjoy a second life as an ordinary pan that can be used like a cast-iron enamelled pan.
www.green-pan.com

TRADITIONAL NON-STICK

Scanpan's reputation for hard-wearing performance precedes it. I find these Danish pans will perform over a long period of time.
www.inthehaus.co.uk

For a good traditional non-stick pan, I would recommend Le Creuset's toughened non-stick range that is PFOA-free. The pans themselves are sturdy heavy-gauge forged aluminium, and as well-made as the cast-ironware that we associate with this name.
www.lecreuset.co.uk

Meat thermometer

It took me a long time to embrace a meat thermometer, but they are indispensible in particular for joints of roast beef, pork and lamb. The Superfast Thermapen lives up to its name, with an accurate digital reading within seconds of being inserted.
www.thermapen.co.uk

Salad spinner

The OXO Good Grips salad spinner with its pump action and brake is a piece of genius design. Every consideration has been built into this kitchen staple. The mini spinner is perfect for low carb snacking: small enough to fit into the fridge, it washes and dries just enough leaves for 1–2 servings, which keep fresh when stored in the inner basket.
www.oxouk.com

Spices

When you move away from enriching food with cream, butter and cheese, the role played by aromatics becomes ever more crucial to the quality of a dish. Whether it is through the addition of fresh herbs, using a good olive oil in a salad, or sourcing the very finest spices.

I am a huge fan of the online spice merchant Seasoned Pioneers, whose spices are handmade and dry-roasted, and all their blends authentic. Conveniently, these come in small lightweight resealable packets, and they will ship anywhere in the world.
www.seasonedpioneers.co.uk

MIRACLE SOUPS

Soups are miraculous for the comforting nourishment they provide, the way they will sustain you without being overly rich, and the fact that they come loaded with goodness. Had it not been quite so unappetising, the idea of a cabbage soup that one could live on and lose weight was quite appealing – the Miracle Cabbage Soup Diet. I do recall a trend for it as a teenager, when being able to squeeze into an ever-tighter pair of jeans was such a cherished goal that, yes, a week of soapy cabbage soup was almost worth it. But why cabbage? Pretty much any vegetable soup qualifies here, and this collection is based on low carb vegetables. I would happily dish these up to friends coming over to supper, and under each basic recipe I have made suggestions for dressing them up, little flourishes, but they are just as good without.

I always try to have a vegetable soup on the go in the fridge; I make it once in a while and freeze it in batches. Many can be dipped into cold, but otherwise a small warming bowl for elevenses or for tea is just what you need to take the edge off your hunger. It's a great snack food. So I think soup as a genre deserves its accolade.

Curried chicken and coconut soup

This satisfies the cravings for a chicken curry, but it can also be eked out with rice or noodles for those who want the full-on experience. I find low- or reduced-fat coconut milk is preferable to the full-fat version in a soup as it strikes a note of luxury without being overly rich.

Serves 6

sea salt

900g–1kg free-range chicken thighs and drumsticks

2 banana shallots, peeled, halved and thinly sliced

2 garlic cloves, peeled and finely chopped

1 medium-hot green chilli, core and seeds discarded, and cut into thin strips 1–2cm long

1 rounded teaspoon Goan curry powder (eg Seasoned Pioneers, see page 14)

400g leeks (trimmed weight), sliced

1 x 400ml can 'light' coconut milk

2 tablespoons lime juice

a large handful coarsely chopped coriander, plus extra to serve

Preheat the oven to 160°C fan/180°C electric/gas 4. Heat a large cast-iron casserole over a medium heat, season the chicken pieces with salt and colour on either side, then remove them to a bowl. You should be able to do this in a single batch. Add the shallots and fry in the rendered fat for a minute or so, stirring frequently, until softened and lightly coloured, then add the garlic and chilli and continue to fry briefly until fragrant. Stir in the curry powder and fry for a moment longer. Stir in 600ml water, season with salt, then return the chicken to the pan, bring to the boil, cover and cook in the oven for 1½ hours, stirring in the leeks halfway through.

Remove the chicken pieces and shred the flesh using a knife and fork, discarding the skin and bones. Stir the meat back into the soup base, then add the coconut milk and a little salt and gently reheat, without allowing the soup to boil. Stir in the lime juice and coriander and serve in warm bowls scattered with coriander.

Carbohydrate 4.2g Protein 26.4g

Broccoli and sun-dried tomato soup

The secret savour here is sun-dried tomatoes, not an ingredient that we tend to associate with soups, but they provide an added dimension with a lovely piquancy and texture. And, should you happen to be making this soup in the middle of winter, then it will carry with it something of the taste of summer.

Serves 4

2 tablespoons extra virgin olive oil
25g unsalted butter
1 onion, peeled and chopped
75g sun-dried tomatoes in oil, drained and sliced
2 garlic cloves, peeled and finely chopped
a small pinch of crushed dried chillies
400g long-stem broccoli, ends trimmed and coarsely sliced
sea salt
1 litre chicken or vegetable stock

Heat the oil and butter in a large saucepan over a medium heat and fry the onion for about 5 minutes, stirring frequently until softened, adding the sun-dried tomatoes, garlic and chilli halfway through. Add the broccoli and some salt, and fry for another few minutes, again stirring frequently. Pour in the stock, bring to the boil and simmer over a low heat for 10 minutes. Transfer to a food processor and whizz the soup to a textured purée. Serve the soup in warm bowls.
Carbohydrate 8.6g Protein 12.4g

WITH PANCETTA
As ever, a drizzle of olive oil finishes this soup off and, even better, some crispy pancetta.

While the soup is cooking, heat the grill and cook 8 **rashers rindless smoked** or **unsmoked pancetta** or **streaky bacon** on both sides until golden and crisp. Serve a couple of rashers in the centre of each bowl of soup.
Carbohydrate 8.6g Protein 18.6g

Cauliflower and mustard seed soup

Cauliflower makes for a beautifully aromatic and silky soup, and I am always amazed at just how little you need do to this vegetable to reap rewards. It is as though it has been hiding its light under a bushel, and puréeing reveals hidden depths of charm and flavour. Here you have the delicate crunch of mustard seeds, stirred in at the very end.

This one is comparatively virtuous for a creamed soup, as so many come loaded with cream, but here that lovely buttery savour is built into it with the initial glazing. Sometimes, by cooking a vegetable in this fashion, it tastes much richer than it would if you added the same amount of butter or oil at the end.

Serves 4

25g unsalted butter
1 tablespoon extra virgin olive oil
2 onions, peeled and chopped
550–600g cauliflower florets
   (1 medium cauli)
800ml chicken or vegetable stock
3 strips of lemon zest, removed with
   a potato peeler
sea salt
2 heaped teaspoons grainy mustard

Heat the butter with the olive oil in a medium saucepan over a medium heat and fry the onions for 4–5 minutes, stirring occasionally, until softened and glossy and just starting to colour. Add the cauliflower florets and fry for another couple of minutes, again stirring occasionally. Add the stock, lemon zest and some salt, bring to the boil, cover and simmer over a low heat for 10 minutes.

Discard the strips of lemon zest then purée the soup in batches in a liquidiser and either transfer to a bowl or a clean pan. Stir or whisk in the mustard, taste and season with a little more salt if necessary. Serve in warm bowls.
Carbohydrate 9.4g Protein 12.1g

WITH HERBS
Drizzle with **extra virgin olive oil** and serve scattered with finely chopped **flat-leaf parsley** or snipped **chives**.
Carbohydrate 9.4g Protein 12.1g

Parsley and celeriac soup with poached egg

A poached egg with a runny yolk that oozes into the soup turns an austere bowl into something almost decadent, and parsley and egg have a particular affinity. But, as ever, you can serve the soup on its own or with a drizzle of oil, if it's not a poached egg kind of occasion, and you are after something simpler.

This is, incidentally, the first outing of celeriac, which you will be seeing a lot of in the coming pages. Apart from being one of my all-time favourites, it is any low carber's best friend in the absence of potatoes. Endless potential.

Serves 6

20g unsalted butter
2 tablespoons extra virgin olive oil
3 large onions, peeled and chopped
900g celeriac (600–700g prepared weight), trimmed and coarsely chopped
225ml white wine
1.4 litres chicken stock
sea salt, black pepper
100g flat-leaf parsley, leaves and very fine stalks

Heat the butter and olive oil in a large saucepan over a medium–low heat and fry the onions for 6–7 minutes, stirring occasionally, until glossy and softened, without allowing them to colour. Add the celeriac and fry for 1 minute longer, stirring to coat it in the butter, then add the wine and simmer until well reduced. Add the stock and some seasoning, bring to the boil, cover and cook over a low heat for 20 minutes or until the celeriac is tender.

Stir in the parsley, submerging it beneath the liquid and simmer for 1 minute longer. Purée the soup in batches in a food processor until fairly smooth and flecked with the green of the herb. If necessary, gently reheat and ladle into warm bowls.
Carbohydrate 13.7g Protein 10.1g

WITH POACHED EGG AND PARMESAN
Fill a large saucepan with water and bring it to the boil. Add a good slug of **white wine** or **cider vinegar**. Now turn down the heat and keep the water at a trembling simmer.

Gently stir the water into a whirlpool using a large spoon and drop in 6 **large eggs**, breaking each one into a teacup first. After about 2 minutes they will rise to the surface, cook them for a further 2 minutes and then remove them using a slotted spoon, trimming off stray tendrils of white against the side of the saucepan. Drop an egg into each bowl of soup, and serve with **extra virgin olive oil** and grated **Parmesan** if wished.
Carbohydrate 13.7g Protein 17.6g

Double celery soup

I've always loved the idea of layering a flavour by using the ingredient in different forms, so a mushroom soup boosted by dried mushrooms, raspberries highlighted with a splash of raspberry eau-de-vie, or apples with Calvados. Here celery and celeriac enhance one another, making for a great double act – the sticks provide bite, the roots provide texture. I suppose you could also season it with a suspicion of that elusive vintage spice, celery salt, to travel even further along the path.

Serves 4

50g unsalted butter
1 onion, peeled and chopped
8 inner sticks of celery (from a whole head), trimmed and sliced
900g celeriac (600–700g prepared weight), trimmed and cut into 2–3cm dice
150ml white wine
800ml vegetable stock
sea salt, black pepper

Melt the butter in a large saucepan over a medium–low heat and fry the onion and celery for about 10 minutes, stirring occasionally, until glossy and softened. Add the celeriac and continue to fry for a further 10 minutes, again stirring occasionally. Add the wine and simmer until well reduced, then add the vegetable stock and some seasoning. Bring to the boil, cover and simmer over a low heat for 15 minutes. Purée the soup in batches in a liquidiser and press through a sieve into a clean saucepan. If necessary, reheat the soup, and ladle into warm bowls.
Carbohydrate 12.1g Protein 4.1g

FAIT SIMPLE
Scatter with finely chopped **chives, parsley** or **celery leaves**.
Carbohydrate 12.1g Protein 4.1g

WITH A LITTLE BLUE CHEESE
Blend 100g **sour cream** and 1 tablespoon **whole milk** in a small bowl. Swirl the soup with the cream, first scatter 100g crumbled **Roquefort** along the length of each swirl, and then some finely chopped **chives**.
Carbohydrate 13.2g Protein 9.9g

Potage bonne femme

This is one of those soups that I could happily live off and often do, especially when feeling in any way delicate. Usually *Potage bonne femme* includes potatoes but it isn't missing anything without – if anything, it has even more flavour from the additional vegetables. There is also enough butter in this recipe to pass on the cream.

In Normandy, where we have a farmhouse, we have access to the *carottes de Créances*, which are grown beside the sea on the Cotentin peninsula in sandy soil that still coats the fat roots when you buy them. Famed for their sweetness and depth of flavour, they make a truly fab soup. If you combine them with the stock from the Christmas turkey, you probably have the pinnacle here. But, at other times of the year, seek out big fat carrots and opt for a homemade stock.

Serves 6

500g carrots, trimmed, peeled
    and sliced
500g leeks (trimmed weight),
    about 6, sliced
1 teaspoon soft lemon thyme leaves
sea salt, black pepper
50g salted butter, diced
200ml white wine
1.2 litres chicken or vegetable stock

Combine the carrots and leeks in a large saucepan. Scatter over the thyme and 2 teaspoons of salt, dot with the butter and pour over the wine.

Bring to the boil, then cover and simmer over a medium heat for 8 minutes. Give the vegetables a stir, turn up the heat to high and cook, uncovered, until all the wine has evaporated. Add the stock, bring to the boil and simmer for 5 minutes. For a textured soup with a little bite, which is my preference, transfer the contents of the pan in batches to a food processor and reduce to a purée or, if you prefer it smooth, use a liquidiser. Return the soup to the saucepan, reheat and season with black pepper, and a little more salt if necessary. Serve in warm bowls.
Carbohydrate 11g Protein 8g

WITH HERBS
Serve scattered with a little chopped **flat-leaf parsley** or **chervil**.
Carbohydrate 11g Protein 8g

Spicy root veg soup

Jane Grigson's curried parsnip soup is famously good and has become part of our national culinary repertoire. It's a formula to be tinkered with, the combination of sweet and mealy vegetables with spices can be wheeled out to any other comforting wintery roots, with fewer carbs than parsnips.

Serves 6

50g unsalted butter
1 onion, peeled and chopped
2 leeks, trimmed and sliced
400g swede, skin cut off and chopped
400g carrots, trimmed, peeled and thickly sliced
sea salt
2 garlic cloves, peeled and finely chopped
1 rounded teaspoon Indonesian curry powder
1.1 litres chicken or vegetable stock
a squeeze of lemon juice

Melt the butter in a large saucepan over a low heat. Add the onion, leeks, swede and carrots, sprinkle over 1 heaped teaspoon of sea salt and fry for 30 minutes, stirring frequently to prevent the vegetables colouring, and stirring in the garlic and curry powder a few minutes before the end.

Pour in the stock, bring to the boil and simmer over a low heat for 15 minutes. Purée the soup in batches using a liquidiser, add a squeeze of lemon juice then taste to check the seasoning. Serve in warm bowls.
Carbohydrate 12g Protein 7.4g

WITH APPLE CHUTNEY
Combine 150g **natural yogurt**, a peeled and coarsely grated **eating apple**, a heaped tablespoon finely chopped **mint** and a little **sea salt** in a bowl, cover and chill until required. This can be made up to a couple of hours in advance. Serve dolloped in the centre of the soup, scattered with a few tiny **mint leaves**.
Carbohydrate 16.3g Protein 9g

Courgette, watercress and mint soup

Frying the courgettes to a deep golden hue brings out the sweetness in this vegetable. It also reduces to a luxuriously silky texture that accounts for the body of the soup, which assumes a rich creaminess that belies its healthy profile, while a mass of watercress and fresh mint added at the very end is both sprightly and fresh.

Serves 4

4 tablespoons extra virgin olive oil
3 leeks, trimmed and sliced
500g courgettes, trimmed and sliced
150ml white wine
900ml chicken stock
sea salt, black pepper
100g watercress
a few mint leaves, plus a little
    finely chopped, to serve

Heat a tablespoon of oil in a large saucepan over a medium heat, add the leeks and fry for about 5 minutes, stirring frequently, until softened and starting to colour, then remove to a bowl. You will need to fry the courgettes in batches, so add another tablespoon of oil to the pan and fry about a third of the courgettes for about 5 minutes, stirring frequently, until softened and lightly golden. Transfer these to the bowl with the leeks and cook the remaining courgettes in the same way.

Return all the vegetables to the saucepan, add the wine and simmer until well reduced, then add the stock and some seasoning, bring to the boil and simmer for 10 minutes. Add the watercress to the soup and simmer for 1 minute longer, then transfer to a food processor, if necessary in batches, add the mint leaves, and whizz to a textured purée. If necessary, gently reheat then ladle into warm bowls and scatter with a little finely chopped mint.
Carbohydrate 6.7g Protein 11.1g

WITH YOGURT
Dress this up with a spoonful of **yogurt** before scattering with a little finely chopped **mint**.
Carbohydrate 7.9g Protein 12g

Rustic pumpkin vichyssoise

Textured soups are, somehow, particularly comforting and nourishing, perhaps because they give you a sense of eating real food as opposed to simply drinking a liquid. This one has everything you would expect from a vichyssoise (leeks and chicken stock sharpened by a little wine), with pumpkin standing in for the potatoes.

Serves 6

50g unsalted butter
500g leeks (trimmed weight), sliced
1 large onion, peeled and chopped
200ml white wine
400g pumpkin flesh (about 600g whole), diced
1.2 litres fresh chicken or vegetable stock
sea salt, black pepper
2 handfuls coarsely chopped flat-leaf parsley, plus extra to serve

Melt the butter in a large saucepan over a medium–low heat and fry the leeks and onion for 8–10 minutes, stirring occasionally, until they are silky and soft without colouring. Pour in the wine and reduce until syrupy. Add the pumpkin to the pan, stir it around for a minute, then add the stock and some seasoning. Bring to the boil and simmer for 10 minutes.

Briefly whizz the soup in batches in a food processor with the parsley, just enough to break up the vegetables – there should be visible nibs of pumpkin. Return it to a clean saucepan, taste to check the seasoning and gently reheat. Serve in warm bowls, scattered with a little extra parsley.
Carbohydrate 8.9g Protein 8.5g

WITH A FLOURISH
Scatter with coarsely chopped **flat-leaf parsley**, with or without a dollop of **low-fat crème fraîche**.
Carbohydrate 10.7g Protein 9.7g

Chilled watermelon and cucumber soup

This is just a little bit pinker and prettier than a classic gazpacho, with watermelon in place of tomatoes. As with the gazpacho on page 30, you can add a teaspoon of sugar.

Serves 4

2 cucumbers, ends discarded, peeled and chopped (about 500g trimmed weight)
500g seeded watermelon flesh, chopped
1 teaspoon chopped shallot
3 tablespoons lemon juice
100ml extra virgin olive oil
1–2 rounded teaspoons sea salt

Purée all the ingredients in a liquidiser, then pass through a sieve into a bowl, cover and chill for at least a couple of hours.
Carbohydrate 11g Protein 1.5g

WITH CHIVES
Serve with a drizzle of **extra virgin olive oil**, scattered with finely chopped **chives**.
Carbohydrate 11g Protein 1.6g

Spinach soup with roasted garlic cream

The deep pea-green of a spinach soup is deliciously dramatic, this one is a mélange of spring onions and watercress. Some crispy lardons and a poached egg (see page 23) would be other good asides, especially in tandem with the garlic cream. Why not?

Serves 4

3 tablespoons extra virgin olive oil
2 bunches of spring onions (about
    125g each), trimmed and sliced
800ml chicken stock
sea salt, black pepper
500g spinach
100g watercress

Heat the oil in a large saucepan over a medium heat, add the spring onions and fry for 5–7 minutes, stirring occasionally, until softened and glossy without colouring. Add the chicken stock and some seasoning, bring to the boil and add the spinach in several goes, pushing it down into the liquid to submerge it, along with the watercress. Bring the stock back to the boil, then cover and simmer over a low heat for 5 minutes. Purée the soup in batches in a liquidiser. Return to the pan and taste to check the seasoning. If necessary, reheat then serve in warm bowls.
Carbohydrate 4.1g Protein 11.3g

WITH ROASTED GARLIC CREAM
An hour or two in advance of eating, preheat the oven to 200°C fan/220°C electric/gas 7 and roast a large **head of garlic** for 30 minutes, then set aside until it is cool enough to handle, or leave to cool completely.

Just before eating, squeeze the cloves from the husk into a small saucepan. Add a tablespoon of **extra virgin olive oil**, 75g **low-fat crème fraîche**, 1 teaspoon of **Madeira** or **medium sherry** if wished, a pinch of **sea salt** and simmer for about a minute, mashing the garlic into the cream until it enriches and thickens slightly.

Serve the soup with a swirl of warm garlic cream, and a little more **extra virgin olive oil** drizzled over if wished.
Carbohydrate 7g Protein 13g

Roast tomato gazpacho

A speedy tomato soup that requires no simmering or chopping – just pop a tray of tomatoes on the vine into a hot oven and you're pretty much there. You could eat it without further ado, but add in a cooling cucumber salsa and you have a gazpacho of sorts. For those not counting carbs, you can also add a teaspoon of sugar to the soup.

Serves 4

1.5kg tomatoes on the vine
5 garlic cloves, unpeeled
6 tablespoons extra virgin olive oil
sea salt, black pepper
1 teaspoon balsamic vinegar

1 cucumber, peeled, halved and
    deseeded, cut into 1cm dice
1 baby red or yellow pepper, cut
    into 1cm-long fine strips
1 tablespoon finely chopped red
    onion
1 tablespoon extra virgin olive oil
1 tablespoon lemon or lime juice
sea salt
coarsely chopped coriander, to serve

Preheat the oven to 220°C fan/240°C electric/gas 9. Arrange the tomatoes in a large roasting dish in a single layer with the garlic cloves, drizzle over 3 tablespoons of oil and roast for 20 minutes. Once they are cool enough to handle, pinch the tomatoes off the vines, squeeze the garlic from its casing and tip these into a liquidiser with any roasting juices. Add a good dose of salt, some black pepper, the vinegar and the remaining oil, and liquidise. Pass through a sieve into a bowl, cover, leave to cool and then chill.
Carbohydrate 12.9g Protein 3.1g

WITH SALSA
You can prepare and combine the vegetables for the salsa in advance, cover and set aside. Shortly before serving, toss them with the oil, the lemon or lime juice and some salt. Serve this spooned over the soup, scattered with a little coriander.
Carbohydrate 14.4g Protein 3.6g

ELEGANT EGGS

Early mornings can present a challenge to those avoiding breakfast cereal, toast and croissants. And not everyone has a taste for salmon teriyaki first thing, so a full egg rack is the gateway to breakfast nirvana. I am hopeless at the French-style of rolled omelette, and it is much more likely to be a Spanish *revueltos*, also known as a 'Chloe Moretz Omelette' in our house (move over Arnold Bennett) on account of a Youtube clip. A friendly cross between scrambled eggs and an omelette, fold the cooked ingredient of your choice such as shreds of ham hock, fried mushrooms or diced asparagus into a couple of seasoned beaten eggs, and scramble in a very hot frying pan with a trickle of olive oil.

Frittatas too, work wonders for the confidence of the butter-fingered, designed to be eaten cold as well as hot. If you don't have time in the morning, make it the day before and you have suitable grazing on which to start the day. I cannot live without a Spanish tortilla, but all those potatoes – hence the recipe that follows, made with celeriac which goes beautifully with Parma ham, and olives as the day wears on.

Eggs too answer the call for a protein snack throughout the day. This could be quails' eggs for dipping into sea salt, or a fried egg with a dash of chilli sauce, while egg mayonnaise turns any *crudité* into a treat, crisp leaves of lettuce heart especially, with a sliver of anchovy.

SNACKS

Quails' eggs and sea salt

Soft-boiled quails' eggs that take up the odd ethereal flake or two of Maldon sea salt when lightly dipped, are a great teatime favourite in this house, or late teatime panned out with olives and gherkins. Actually anytime. And just in case you are new to quails' eggs, there is an art to peeling them – by gently rolling a cooked egg on the surface of the table, which crackles its shell before breaking the membrane and peeling it off with the shell.

Allow about 4 **quails' eggs** per person. Bring a pan of water to the boil and gently lower in the quails' eggs (if cooking more than a couple of dozen this is easiest done in two goes), and boil for 2½ minutes to leave them wet in the centre, or 3 minutes if you prefer them hard-boiled, assuming they weigh in at about 14–15g. (I have been taken aback by the quails' eggs in France that are double the size of the ones I am accustomed to cooking.) Drain and refill the pan with cold water to stop the yolk cooking any further. **Sea salt** at the ready.
Carbohydrate 0g Protein 7.2g

Fried egg and chilli sauce

A slightly louche snack, but ultimately rather healthy, especially if you throw in a few small lettuce leaves. Fried eggs are a great cause for debate – I like to fry the white to a lacy crisp around the edges before flipping the egg momentarily to seal the top of the yolk that remains runny within.

For a snack for one, heat a tablespoon of **groundnut** or **vegetable oil** in a non-stick frying pan over a medium–high heat. Break in an **egg**, season with **sea salt** and **black pepper** and fry for about 2 minutes until golden on the underside and the edges look lacy and crisp. Carefully turn with a spatula and cook the yolk side for about 10 seconds, then slip onto a plate and serve with **chilli sauce**.
Carbohydrate 0.2g Protein 6.9g

Egg mayonnaise salad cups

You don't have to be avoiding carbs to make small lettuce heart leaves filled with egg mayonnaise, one of the best hand-me-rounds or snacks. I wheel these out endlessly at drinks parties, picnics, teas, any excuse, it's the best bit of the sandwich without the bread.

Makes about 24

**3 chicory heads, red or green,
    or 2–4 Little Gem lettuces**

Egg mayonnaise:
6 medium eggs
4 heaped tablespoons mayonnaise
sea salt, black pepper

Cut the base off the chicory heads or lettuces, discard the outer leaves, and separate out the remainder, reserving the small heart for some other use and also any particularly large leaves. You should get about 8 from each head of chicory, and 4–8 from lettuce heads.

Boil the eggs for 9–10 minutes in a small pan of water, then drain and refill the pan with cold water and leave them to cool. Shell the eggs, discarding 2 of the whites, and mash the remainder quite finely in a bowl using a fork. Add the mayo and some seasoning and blend. You can make this well in advance, in which case cover and chill it.

Up to an hour or so in advance of eating drop a teaspoon of the egg mayo in the centre of each salad leaf.
Carbohydrate 0.6g Protein 1.7g

WITH BACON
Fry 100g **lardons** in their rendered fat in a large, non-stick frying pan over a medium heat until golden, stirring occasionally. Drain them on a double thickness of kitchen paper and leave to cool.

Scatter some finely sliced **spring onion** over the egg mayonnaise and a few lardons, or if these are particularly chunky, just one.
Carbohydrate 0.6g Protein 2.4g

WITH MUSTARD AND CRESS
Scatter the filled leaves with ½ punnet **mustard and cress**.
Carbohydrate 0.6g Protein 1.7g

Egg wraps

Tortillas are out of bounds, but these wafer-thin omelettes make a fine substitute, and you can roll them up with any of your favourite fillings, from smoked salmon and cream cheese to shredded duck and cucumber. There are two versions, a slightly jazzier spicy one and a plain one that is great for turning out in a matter of minutes.

Serves 4

4 medium eggs
1 tablespoon lemon juice
3 heaped tablespoons coarsely chopped coriander leaves
sea salt
1 tablespoon vegetable oil, plus extra for the frying pan
1 teaspoon finely chopped fresh ginger
1 garlic clove, peeled and finely chopped
1 heaped teaspoon finely chopped medium-hot green chilli

SPICY WRAPS
Whisk the eggs, lemon juice, coriander and a little salt in a medium bowl. Heat the tablespoon of oil in a small saucepan over a medium heat and fry the ginger, garlic and chilli until the garlic just starts to colour, then whisk this into the eggs.

Brush a 24cm non-stick frying pan with vegetable oil, place over a medium heat and fry a quarter of the egg mixture at a time as if making pancakes. Cook the omelettes for about 1 minute or until dry on the surface, then use a spatula to turn and cook on the other side for another 30–45 seconds. Leave to cool.

– Eat on their own, or serve as an accompaniment to a curry, cut into strips.

– Spread with **quark** or **low-fat soft cheese**, scatter over some **alfalfa** and roll up.

– Arrange some shredded **roast duck** about a third of the way across the wrap, top with fine strips of **cucumber**, **red pepper** and **spring onion**, and roll up.
Wraps only: Carbohydrate 0.4g Protein 6.6g

PLAIN WRAPS
Whisk together 4 medium **eggs**, 1 tablespoon of **extra virgin olive oil**, 1 tablespoon of **water** and some **sea salt** and **black pepper**, and cook as above.

– Spread generously with **quark** or **low-fat soft cheese**, lay a slice of **roast ham** and some **watercress sprigs** or **mustard and cress** on top and roll up.

– Spread with **low-fat soft cheese**, lay some sliced **smoked salmon** on top, squeeze over a little **lemon juice** and grind over some **black pepper**. Scatter over some shredded **spinach** leaves and roll up.

– Spread with **black or green tapenade**, arrange some cooked **asparagus spears** in a line about a third of the way across, scatter over some quartered **cherry tomatoes**, and roll up.
Wraps only: Carbohydrate 0.3g Protein 6.3g

Smoked salmon and spring onion frittata

You could also make this with crabmeat if you have a good supply of it, and this does seem to be getting easier, using a mixture of white and brown meat seasoned with a little salt.

Serves 4

200g sliced smoked salmon
6 slim spring onions, trimmed and
    finely sliced
6 medium eggs
juice of ½ lemon, plus ½ teaspoon
    finely grated lemon zest
2 teaspoons finely chopped
    medium-hot red chilli
3 tablespoons coarsely chopped
    flat-leaf parsley
2 tablespoons extra virgin olive oil

Cut out any dark flesh from the smoked salmon, halve the slices along the central line and cut across into strips about 2cm wide.

Reserving a tablespoon of the spring onions, whisk the eggs with the lemon juice and zest, the chilli, the remaining spring onions and parsley in a large bowl, then fold in the smoked salmon, separating out the strips.

Place a 24cm non-stick frying pan with a heatproof handle over a medium heat for several minutes and at the same time preheat an overhead grill.
Add a tablespoon of olive oil to the pan, tip in the omelette mixture, evenly distributing the salmon and cook for 3 minutes. Scatter over the reserved spring onions and drizzle over another tablespoon of oil, and place the pan under the grill for 3–4 minutes. I like this best at room temperature.
Carbohydrate 0.5g Protein 22.4g

Goat's cheese frittata

Goat's cheese frittata is twenty-first-century speak for a cheese omelette, with deliciously crispy edges and gooey pockets of cheese, one for partnering with a tomato salad and a few salad leaves.

Serves 4

8 medium eggs
sea salt, black pepper
150g medium-mature goat's cheese,
    cut into 1cm dice
2 tablespoons finely chopped chives
2 tablespoons extra virgin olive oil
15g unsalted butter

Preheat the oven to 220°C fan/240°C electric/gas 9. Whisk the eggs with some seasoning in a bowl, then fold in the goat's cheese and chives. Heat the olive oil in a 24cm frying pan with a heatproof handle over a medium heat and, once it is hot, tip in the eggs. Scramble rapidly using a fork for about 30 seconds until they are half set. Remove the pan from the heat, dot the butter over the surface of the frittata and place in the oven for 5–6 minutes by which time it should be firm, puffed up and lightly golden.

Serve the frittata in quarters.
Carbohydrate 0.7g Protein 17.5g

WITH HAM
Serve a slice of **honey roast ham** loosely piled at the tip of each wedge.
Carbohydrate 1g Protein 19.9g

Courgette frittata

Here grilled baby courgettes star in a simple frittata, with basil and Parmesan. If baby ones aren't available I would have a play around with larger ones, but given how easily they grow it may well be one of those allotment vegetables you are able to harvest in miniature.

Serves 4

350g baby courgettes, ends
    trimmed and halved lengthways
4 tablespoons extra virgin olive oil
sea salt, black pepper
6 medium eggs
50g freshly grated Parmesan,
    plus 25g finely sliced
a large handful of basil leaves,
    torn in half
25g finely sliced Parmesan

Heat a ridged griddle over a medium heat for several minutes. Place the halved courgettes in a large bowl, drizzle over 2 tablespoons of olive oil, add some seasoning and toss to coat them. If you are using a single griddle then you will need to cook the courgettes in two batches. Lay them out in a single layer, turn them as they colour on the underside and cook the second side. Remove them to a plate, they don't have to be completely cool before the next stage, but equally can be cooked in advance if wished.

Whisk the eggs in a bowl, then stir in the grated Parmesan, basil leaves and some seasoning. Fold in the griddled courgettes. Place a 24cm non-stick frying pan with a heatproof handle over a medium heat for several minutes and at the same time preheat an overhead grill. Add a tablespoon of oil to the pan, tip in the egg and courgette mixture and cook for 3 minutes. Scatter the Parmesan slices over the top of the omelette, drizzle over another tablespoon of oil and place under the grill for 3–4 minutes until golden and puffy at the sides. The frittata can be eaten hot or at room temperature.

Carbohydrate 2.3g Protein 18g

Spinach and Parma ham frittata

This deepish spinach omelette is topped with slivers of Parma ham that turn crispy under the grill.

Serves 4

3–4 tablespoons extra virgin olive oil
3 garlic cloves, peeled and finely
　　chopped
500g spinach leaves, washed and
　　dried
sea salt, black pepper
4 medium eggs
freshly grated nutmeg
100g quark
4 slices Parma or other air-dried
　　ham, halved into long strips

Heat a tablespoon of oil in a 24cm non-stick frying pan with a heatproof handle over a high heat, add half the garlic and, once it is sizzling and fragrant, add about a quarter of the spinach. Toss until this collapses a little then add another quarter of spinach. Season and cook until it has wilted. Transfer the spinach to a sieve and press out as much of the liquid as possible, then transfer it to a bowl and prepare the remaining spinach in the same fashion.

Whisk the eggs in a large bowl with a little nutmeg, add the spinach and a little more seasoning and stir to amalgamate everything.

Preheat an overhead grill on high, and return the same frying pan in which you cooked the spinach to a medium heat. It may already be coated in oil from cooking the spinach, but otherwise add a tablespoon to the pan, tip in the spinach mixture and cook for 3 minutes. In the meantime, dot with the quark, then drape the slices of Parma ham over and gently press down to level the quark underneath a little. Drizzle over a tablespoon of oil and place the pan under the grill for 3–4 minutes. Serve the frittata hot or at room temperature.
Carbohydrate 3.9g Protein 17g

Moussey omelette

This omelette is a low carb solution to a soufflé, which relies on flour, butter and more cheese.

Serves 2

5 large egg yolks, and 3 egg whites
sea salt, black pepper
25g freshly grated Parmesan
10g unsalted butter

Preheat the grill. Whisk the egg yolks with some seasoning in a large bowl. Stiffly whisk the egg whites using an electric whisk and fold them in two goes into the yolks, including the Parmesan with the final addition. Heat a 24cm non-stick frying pan over a low heat. Add the butter and turn the heat up, once it foams add the omelette mixture, spreading it out with a spoon. Cook for 1 minute, then place under the grill for a further minute until lightly golden. Loosen the edges, fold the omelette in half and halve it onto two warmed plates.
Carbohydrate 0.4g Protein 18.6g

WITH BACON
Just before cooking the omelette, preheat the grill and cook 4 **slices rindless unsmoked streaky bacon** until crisp on either side.
Carbohydrate 0.4g Protein 24.8g

Simple Spanish tortilla

Spanish omelettes can be made with all manner of vegetables, but the classic potato and onion tortilla has to be the most comforting. It is hard to guess that this isn't the real thing – it certainly disappears with the same speed – and has the same potential of being dressed up with air-dried ham and olives, or eaten as part of a selection of Mediterranean appetisers.

Serves 4

extra virgin olive oil
500g celeriac, skin cut off, cut
  downwards into wedges and
  sliced 0.5cm thick
sea salt, black pepper
2 onions, peeled, halved and sliced
6 medium eggs
1 heaped tablespoon fresh lemon
  thyme leaves

Heat 2 tablespoons of olive oil in a 24cm non-stick frying pan with a heatproof handle over a medium heat, add the celeriac and cook for about 5 minutes, turning it now and again, until it is coated in the oil. Season with salt, drizzle 2 tablespoons of water over the veg, cover the pan with a large saucepan lid and cook over a low heat for about 5 minutes until just tender; it may be lightly coloured. Using the lid, drain off any excess water and carefully transfer the celeriac to a large bowl.

Wipe out the pan with kitchen paper, return it to a medium heat, add another couple of tablespoons of oil and fry the onions for 7–12 minutes, stirring frequently, until golden, seasoning them at the end. Mix them into the celeriac.

To cook the omelette, whisk the eggs in a bowl with a little seasoning, then pour them onto the celeriac and onions and gently stir to combine. Preheat an overhead grill to high, and return the frying pan in which you cooked the vegetables to a medium heat. This may be coated with oil from frying the onions, but otherwise add a tablespoon of oil to the hot pan, tip in the egg and celeriac mixture, level the surface and cook for 4 minutes.

Scatter the thyme leaves over the top of the omelette, drizzle over another tablespoon of oil and place under the grill for about 3 minutes until golden and sizzling, keeping a careful eye on it to make sure it doesn't burn – if it does seem to be colouring too quickly then move the pan down a little or turn the grill down. It should still be slightly moist in the centre, without being overly runny, but will firm up and cook with the heat of the pan as it cools.
Carbohydrate 8.4g Protein 11.7g

CHOP HOUSE

The pursuit of protein for one or two people provides the perfect excuse to indulge in a lamb chop or a couple of chicken thighs, or to satiate your appetite with a steak. Duck breasts too are ideal.

All of these smaller cuts tend to come with their fair share of fat, as does a decent roast, as it is this element that accounts for the succulence of the meat. Without the fat the flesh would be desiccated and unalluring. But just because you cook meat with its fat, doesn't mean you have to eat meat with its fat. Once it has performed its task, unless you are particularly partial to it (personally I am not), simply remove it. Your dinner will be all the finer for the role it has played.

Chicken and aubergine tagine traybake

A tagine can be a tricky one to eat without lots of flatbread or couscous for mopping. That was ever their *raison d'être*, to make the most of a humble cut by using it to scent a gravy that will stretch to feed a multitude of people, coupled with a large pile of bread to spread the pleasure.

That said, some tagines are relatively dry, fish ones in particular, when their charm is as much to do with the souk they conjure up through their scents as with the gravy and bread. This tagine roast is just as at home with salad leaves, ever clean and sprightly, or a tomato salad. It also makes use of those mixed packs of thighs and drumsticks, that can be more economical mid-week than a whole bird.

Serves 6

1½ teaspoons ground ginger
1½ teaspoons paprika
½ teaspoon ground cumin
about 20 saffron filaments, ground
extra virgin olive oil
6 free-range chicken thighs
6 free-range chicken drumsticks
3 aubergines, cut into slices 1–2cm
    thick, ends discarded
sea salt, black pepper
3 red onions, peeled, halved and
    sliced
100g preserved lemons, thinly
    sliced if baby or chopped if
    large, seeds discarded
coarsely chopped coriander, to serve

Blend the spices with 3 tablespoons of olive oil in a small bowl, brush this over the chicken pieces to coat them, placing them in a large bowl as you go. Cover with clingfilm and chill for at least 1 hour, but preferably several.

Preheat the oven to 190°C fan/210°C electric/gas 7. Place a ridged cast-iron griddle over a medium heat. You will need to cook the aubergine slices in batches. Brush one side of as many slices as will fit on the griddle with olive oil, season and grill for 2–3 minutes until striped with gold, then brush the top side, turn and grill this side too. They should still appear underdone, as they will cook further in the oven. Remove the slices to a plate as they are ready. Now season the chicken pieces on both sides, and grill for 1–2 minutes on either side to colour them – again you will probably need to do this in batches. Toss the onion in a bowl with a couple of tablespoons of olive oil.

Arrange the aubergine, onion and preserved lemons in a couple of roasting dishes (about 25 x 38cm), and nestle the chicken pieces between them, the skin-side of the thighs facing upwards. Drizzle over a little more oil and roast for 35–40 minutes, gently turning the vegetables halfway through with a spatula, leaving the chicken pieces uppermost. By the end of the cooking time the vegetables should be golden and sitting in syrupy juices. Served scattered with coriander.
Carbohydrate 9.3g Protein 71.7g

BARBECUED
Barbecue the **chicken pieces** for 20–40 minutes in total. Make up six 26cm skewers with 2 **aubergines** cut into 3cm cubes, and 2 **red onions** cut into eight pieces each. Drizzle over some **extra virgin olive oil** to coat them, season with **sea salt** and **black pepper** and grill for 20–40 minutes in total, on all four sides. Make a relish with 6 tablespoons of chopped **coriander**, 1 tablespoon of finely chopped **preserved lemon** and 3 tablespoons of **extra virgin olive oil**.
Carbohydrate 5.4g Protein 25.8g

Chicken and red pepper traybake

This is another lovely all-in-one bake, the peppers and onions providing a sweet succulence, so there is no need for any additional sauce. But some pitted olives would be a good addition, or ones stuffed with chilli perhaps, and, however naff, I do love those pimento-stuffed green ones.

Serves 6

6 red or orange peppers, core, seeds
    and membranes removed
2 onions, peeled, halved and sliced
8–10 fresh thyme sprigs
2 bay leaves
5 garlic cloves, peeled and sliced
extra virgin olive oil
sea salt, black pepper
6 free-range chicken breasts, skin on
1 teaspoon balsamic vinegar

Preheat the oven to 180°C fan/200°C electric/gas 6. Quarter the peppers and arrange them, together with the onions, in a crowded single layer in a baking dish or roasting tin (about 25 x 38cm). Tuck in the herbs and scatter over the garlic. Drizzle over 4 tablespoons of olive oil and season with salt and pepper. Roast for 40 minutes, stirring halfway through. Towards the end of this time place a large, non-stick frying pan over a medium heat, cut out the tendon from the underside of each chicken breast, lightly brush all over with olive oil, season, and sear them until golden on both sides. You will need to do this in batches.

Give the peppers a stir to baste them, and nestle the chicken breasts between them, skin-side up. Roast for a further 20–25 minutes until the chicken is golden and sizzling and the peppers are singed at the edges. Drip the vinegar over the peppers, vaguely stirring to mix it into the juices and serve straight away.
Carbohydrate 13.8g Protein 41.3g

Roast chicken thighs with orange and cinnamon

The more I cook with sumac, the more in love I fall. A close friend, the cookery writer Nadeh Saleh, who was brought up in the mountains surrounding Lebanon, tells me it was used in place of lemons in areas where the trees might not flourish. It has to it an elegant sourness in addition to a smoky savour, and its deep-purple hue is exquisite – aubergine with a hint of rust… if only dress fabrics came in the same. It is now quite widely available.

Serves 4

sea salt, black pepper
8 free-range chicken thighs
3 red onions, peeled, halved and
    thinly sliced
5–6 bay leaves
2 x 7cm cinnamon sticks, halved
1 orange, unpeeled, thinly sliced,
    ends discarded
2 tablespoons extra virgin olive oil
powdered sumac

Preheat the oven to 190°C fan/210°C electric/gas 7. Heat a large, non-stick frying pan over a medium–high heat, season and colour the chicken thighs, skin-side first. Do this in two batches, tipping out the excess fat in between.

In the meantime combine the onions, bay leaves, cinnamon sticks and sliced orange in a large roasting dish (about 25 x 38cm). Drizzle over the oil, and tuck in the chicken thighs, skin-side up, once they are ready. Lightly dust the chicken skin with sumac and roast for 40 minutes.
Carbohydrate 10.6g Protein 38.4g

Really juicy chicken breasts with garlic spinach

This slightly, or perhaps very, obscure way of cooking chicken breasts is based on the *recherché* restaurant technique of cooking *sous vide*. This is the rustic take on the method, which, should you do it properly, involves a water bath maintained at a temperature a little higher than you might fancy bathing in. The idea is that the meat or fish is poached very, very slowly, and then finished in a frying pan, giving you the best of both worlds: an exceptionally tender and succulent interior without sacrificing the crisp outside.

Serves 4

extra virgin olive oil
500g spinach, washed and dried
4 free-range chicken breasts, skin on
about 1.5 litres chicken or
	vegetable stock
sea salt, black pepper
3 garlic cloves, peeled and finely
	sliced
1–2 teaspoons finely sliced
	medium-hot red chilli
lemon wedges, to serve

Heat a tablespoon of oil in a large frying pan, add a pile of spinach leaves (you will need to cook them in batches) and toss until they wilt. Remove them to a bowl and proceed with the remainder.

Lay the chicken breasts skin-side down on a board, flatten them with your hands, and cut out the white tendon from the underside if visible.

Bring the stock to the boil in a medium–large saucepan and season with salt. Turn the heat down as low as possible. Immerse the chicken breasts in the stock and cook for 15 minutes, without boiling. Transfer them to a plate and pat dry with kitchen paper. The stock can be used again: first pour it through a fine sieve, discarding any sediment in the base.

Heat ½ tablespoon of oil in a large frying pan over a medium heat, season the chicken breasts well and fry for several minutes on each side until golden. You may need to do this in batches, or use two pans.

Just before the chicken is ready, heat a tablespoon of oil in another frying pan over a medium heat, add the garlic and chilli and cook briefly until fragrant and lightly coloured, then stir in the spinach, season with salt and heat through. Serve the chicken and spinach accompanied by lemon wedges.
Carbohydrate 4.7g Protein 43.6g

Veal chops with sage and lemon

Even though we tend towards 'rose veal' in this country, on ethical grounds, if you shop at a good butcher there is no reason to think that Continental veal will have been less ethically produced than any of its other meat. Production standards in Europe have changed enormously in recent years, and producers of high-quality veal work in close association with animal welfare groups, as do the better meat producers in the UK.

Here you have lots of garlicky butter, lemon juice and sage – delicious with a succulent veal chop. It's a dish for two, but easily doubles up for four if you are happy to have a couple of frying pans on the go. I'd serve some watercress here, or rocket.

Serves 2

2 tablespoons extra virgin olive oil
sea salt, black pepper
2 veal chops (about 150g each)
30g unsalted butter
3 garlic cloves, peeled and smashed
a handful of sage leaves
juice of ½ lemon

Heat the oil in a large, non-stick frying pan over a medium heat, season the chops and fry them for about 3 minutes on one side until nicely coloured. Turn them, add the butter and garlic and fry for a further few minutes, until the meat is nicely caramelised on the outside and with a slight give when pressed. Scatter the sage leaves into the juices a couple of minutes before the end, and pour over the lemon juice just before removing the pan from the heat. Serve the chops with the juices spooned over and the sage leaves, discarding the garlic.
Carbohydrate 2.1g Protein 28.3g

Lamb chops with coriander, ginger and chilli

These lamb chops are marinated with a handful of aromatics, and I would suggest dishing them up with a green salad that includes avocado, which is particularly good with the pink meat of a tender loin chop, cooked medium-rare. Maybe some Tzatziki (see page 81) and roasted veg (see pages 166–169), too.

Serves 4

Marinade:
4 tablespoons extra virgin olive oil
finely grated zest of 1 lemon, plus
    1 tablespoon juice
3 garlic cloves, peeled and crushed
    to a paste
1 tablespoon finely grated fresh
    ginger
1 heaped teaspoon finely chopped
    medium-hot red chilli
1 teaspoon ground coriander

Lamb:
sea salt, black pepper
4 x 150–180g lamb loin chops

To serve:
coarsely chopped coriander leaves
a few dressed baby salad leaves
slivers of avocado

Make a marinade with the olive oil, lemon zest and juice, garlic, ginger, chilli and ground coriander in a large bowl. Add the chops and coat them in the mixture – you can do this up to a couple of hours before eating, in which case cover and chill.

Heat a large non-stick frying pan over a medium-high heat, season the chops either side and fry them for about 4 minutes on either side to leave them pink in the centre; they should give slightly when pressed without feeling soft. Stand them on their sides to colour the fat, then leave to rest for a few minutes in a warm serving dish. Drain off the fat in the pan, add any leftover marinade and allow it to sizzle off the heat for about 30 seconds, then spoon this over the chops and scatter over some coriander. Serve with a little salad with slivers of avocado.
Carbohydrate 1.4g Protein 22.7g

Lamb steaks with mint and pomegranate

I was a latecomer to lamb steaks, but what a great cut. They remind me of the *côtes de porc* we get out in Normandy, an exclusively French cut of pork steak or chop that comes intricately laced with veins of fat, and is thinly sliced some 2cm thick. I have yet to find an equivalent over here, but lamb steaks will do. This is one of those suppers that can readily be drummed up in that precious half hour between arriving home from work and slumping in front of the telly.

Serves 4

25g mint leaves
extra virgin olive oil
seeds of ½ pomegranate and
    2 tablespoons juice*
a squeeze of lemon juice
sea salt, black pepper
4 lamb steaks, leg or chump (about
    150g–200g each), 2–3cm thick
100g rocket leaves

Put the mint leaves in a food processor with 6 tablespoons of olive oil, the pomegranate juice, lemon juice and some seasoning and whizz to make a textured dressing.

Heat a teaspoon of oil in a large non-stick frying pan over a high heat, season the steaks on either side and fry for 5–6 minutes in total until golden. If they give slightly when pressed without feeling too squashy they are medium-rare. Then stand them on their sides to colour the fat, and remove to a warm plate to rest for a few minutes.

Toss the rocket with olive oil to coat it, and season with a pinch of salt. Place the steaks on serving plates, drizzle with any of the juices given out while they rested, pile the rocket to the side, scatter the pomegranate seeds over the leaves, and drizzle the dressing over both the lamb and the salad.
Carbohydrate 4g Protein 29.9g

---

* TIP: If you extract the seeds working over a bowl, you should collect the necessary juice at the same time.

Lamb chop and watermelon traybake

The idea of roasting watermelon struck me as being on the obscure side of good taste, but I was bowled over when I tried it. The fruit gives out its juices as it roasts which form the basis for a delicious gravy, and the flesh reduces to a silky sunset orange sliver, that you would never recognise as being watermelon.

Serves 4

1kg seeded watermelon flesh, cut into slim segments and then about 5cm wedges
50g salted butter
sea salt, black pepper
8 x 125–150g lamb loin chops
1 tablespoon white balsamic vinegar
a few fresh rosemary needles
1 tablespoon extra virgin olive oil

Preheat the oven to 220°C fan /240°C electric/gas 9. Arrange the watermelon in a large roasting dish (about 25 x 35cm) in a single layer, dot with the butter and season very lightly. Roast for 35–40 minutes, stirring halfway through; as it cooks it will give out copious juices, a little of which may remain at the end of this time.

Towards the end of the roasting time, heat a large non-stick frying pan over a high heat. Season the chops on both sides and sear until nicely golden, including the fat at the edges. You will need to cook these in two batches.

Drizzle the vinegar over the watermelon and give it a stir, loosening it with a spatula. Arrange the chops on top, scatter over a few rosemary needles and drizzle over the oil and return to the oven for 10 minutes. Leave to rest for 5 minutes. There should be a lovely pool of juices to spoon over the lamb and watermelon.
Carbohydrate 18.9g Protein 38.5g

Duck breasts with roast peppers

This way of cooking duck breasts is in line with the method outlined on page 51, and has the same things going for it. It's a great basic, the lean succulence of the meat on a par with rare roast beef.

To spice it up, you could also sprinkle ½ teaspoon each of ground cumin and coriander, and a hint of cayenne pepper over the fat before frying the breasts. And the dish can be eaten hot, warm or at room temperature, whatever suits.

Serves 4

Peppers:
6 long pointed red peppers (about 750g), core and seeds removed, halved lengthways and again across
2 red onions, peeled, halved and sliced
4 tablespoons extra virgin olive oil
sea salt, black pepper
1 tablespoon balsamic vinegar
a handful of basil leaves, torn (optional)

Duck breasts:
4 x 150–200g duck breasts, skin on

Preheat the oven to 180°C fan/200°C electric/gas 6. Arrange the peppers and onions in a roasting tin (about 25 x 38cm). Drizzle over the olive oil, season and toss, then drizzle over the vinegar. Roast for 1 hour, stirring every 20 minutes, until golden and syrupy. Mix in some basil if wished, leaving the peppers to cool first if serving them at room temperature.

Meanwhile, bring a medium pan of water to the boil, and place it over the lowest heat. Score the duck breasts diagonally at 2cm intervals and wrap each one individually in foil. Immerse them in the hot water, and poach a small breast for 10 minutes, and a larger one for 15 minutes to leave them rare, 5 minutes longer than this for medium-rare. Remove the duck breasts from the water, unwrap and pat them dry.

Heat a large non-stick frying pan over a medium–high heat, season the duck breasts well and fry skin-side down for 6–8 minutes until really golden and crisp, pouring off the rendered fat halfway through. Turn and cook the flesh side for 30–60 seconds. Transfer them to a warm plate and leave to rest for 15 minutes, and slice to serve. The breasts should be medium-rare. Serve with the roast peppers.
Carbohydrate 18.2g Protein 27.3g

Lamb chop traybake with aubergine, peppers and mint sauce

This is Anglo-Provençal, lamb chops with mint sauce and roasted Med veg. Relaxed in character and more South of France than Middle England, and as I find it so hard to eat a lamb chop with a knife and fork when the natural thing is to pick it up with your fingers, that only makes it more appealing.

Serves 4

Lamb and veg:
2 red peppers, core and seeds removed, and quartered
extra virgin olive oil
sea salt, black pepper
2 small aubergines, ends discarded and cut into 1cm slices
8 small lamb loin chops (about 125g each)
3 bay leaves

Sauce:
2 teaspoons balsamic vinegar
a pinch of golden caster sugar
1 scant teaspoon Dijon mustard
4 tablespoons extra virgin olive oil
10g finely chopped mint leaves
10g finely chopped basil leaves

Preheat the oven to 190°C fan/210°C electric/gas 7. Arrange the peppers in a large roasting tin (about 25 x 38cm), drizzle over 2 tablespoons of olive oil, season and roast for 30 minutes.

In the meantime, heat a large, non-stick frying pan over a medium–high heat. You will need to cook the aubergine slices in batches. Brush olive oil on both sides of as many slices as will fit into the pan, season just one side and sear until golden either side. Remove to a plate and cook the remainder in the same fashion. Also season the chops on both sides and colour these too, including the fat at the edges. You will need to cook these in two batches.

To prepare the sauce, whisk the vinegar with the sugar, some seasoning and the mustard in a small bowl, then whisk in the oil and stir in the herbs.

Once the peppers are cooked, mix in the aubergine slices and bay leaves and lay the chops on top. Roast for 15 minutes, then leave to stand for 5 minutes. Serve the vegetables and chops with the sauce spooned over.
Carbohydrate 8.4g Protein 39g

Duck and beetroot traybake

There is something about the combination of beetroot and red onions, and here you have a deliciously syrupy mess of an affair where they are cooked in the rendered duck fat and olive oil, with gorgeously pink tender meat.

Serves 4

700g beetroot, peeled and cut into
    thin wedges
extra virgin olive oil
sea salt, black pepper
4 red onions, peeled, halved and
    thinly sliced
6 thick slices fresh ginger
¾ teaspoon five-spice powder
4 duck breasts, skin on
1 tablespoon balsamic vinegar
coarsely chopped flat-leaf parsley,
    to serve

Preheat the oven to 180°C fan/200°C electric/gas 6. Arrange the beetroot in a large roasting pan (about 25 x 38cm), pour over 2 tablespoons of olive oil, season and toss, and cook for 20 minutes.

Scatter the onions and ginger over the beetroot, drizzle over another couple of tablespoons of oil, season and give the vegetables a stir, then roast for a further 25 minutes.

At the same time, heat a large, non-stick frying pan over a high heat. Rub the five-spice powder into the skin of the duck breasts. Season them and fry skin-side down for several minutes until golden, then drain off the fat, turn and briefly sear the flesh side to colour it. You will probably need to cook the breasts in two batches, removing them to a plate as you go.

Drizzle the balsamic vinegar over the vegetables and give them a stir, settle the duck breasts skin-side up between them and roast for a further 15 minutes. Remove the duck breasts to a board and leave to rest for 5 minutes. Discard the ginger, and tip the roasting pan to collect the juices in one corner, then spoon off any excess fat, leaving the ruby beetroot juices behind. Slice the duck breasts, or provide everyone with steak knives. Serve with the vegetables, scattered with parsley.
Carbohydrate 24.4g Protein 26.8g

Minute steaks with griddled asparagus

This is a great way of updating this vegetable: griddled asparagus can be included in all manner of salads, with slow-roasted tomatoes and the like. A double act of thick and thin spears provides a little more interest, but you could use either on their own. Don't be put off if you haven't got a ridged griddle, as a large, non-stick frying pan will do.

Minute steaks make a little go a long way and, true to their name, they are cooked in just that amount of time.

Serves 4

400g finger-thick and fine asparagus spears (trimmed weight)
2 x 250g rump steaks, cut about 3cm thick
extra virgin olive oil
sea salt, black pepper

Bring a large pan of salted water to the boil. Add the finger-thick asparagus spears and cook for 1 minute, then add the fine spears and cook for a further 2 minutes. Drain them into a colander, pass under the cold tap, then set aside.

Slice each steak into two thin steaks, then beat them using a rolling pin to a thickness of a few millimetres. Don't worry if the seams of fat cause them to come apart into smaller steaks.

Heat a ridged cast-iron griddle over a high heat. Brush the steaks with oil and season on either side, then grill them in batches for 30 seconds on each side for medium-rare, or 45–60 seconds if you prefer them medium, pressing down with a spatula to help brand the steaks with stripes. Transfer them to a warm plate and cover with foil to keep warm. Turn the heat down to medium. Toss the asparagus in a large bowl with a couple of tablespoons of oil and some seasoning, and grill in a couple of batches for 2–3 minutes each side until golden, transferring them to the plate with the steak. Serve the steaks with the asparagus spears.
Carbohydrate 2.3g Protein 27.5g

WITH CHEAT'S BEARNAISE
Combine 50g **mayonnaise**, 50g **sour cream**, 50g **zero-fat Greek yogurt**, and 2 heaped teaspoons finely chopped **fresh tarragon** in a small bowl, and season with **sea salt** if necessary. Accompany the steak and the asparagus with the sauce, scattering over a few tarragon leaves.
Carbohydrate 3.6g Protein 29.3g

BURGER BAR

I recall swelling with pride the day my eight-year old told me he hated Macdonald's. This wasn't entirely without encouragement from me, but I certainly didn't throw a hissy fit at the idea of the occasional Happy Meal when he was young, as long as he could find someone else to take him. Of the many reasons to resent this fast-food chain, the one that is uppermost for me is the way that the food corrupts the palate. The pappy buns and insidious fat-soaked sticks that go by the name of fries, are such a far cry from real food, that if you do happen to take to them, then it is likely that the same articles made from scratch using quality ingredients will start to seem like second best to the ersatz thing. Hence a junk-food habit is formed.

When we talk about the obesity epidemic being linked to the rise of fructose or added sugar in processed foods, in lay terms, you could translate this to meaning that many of today's convenience savoury foods are effectively sweet foods with added salt. Take the cheese out of the cheese puff pastry twist in the supermarket bakery, and you are left with a sweetened brioche that would be more at home spread with jam. But it is balanced with enough salt to disguise it. To take account of this increase in the sweetness of savoury foods, with everything being relative, sweet foods are becoming ever more saccharine – some almost aggressively so, it is hard to imagine how distorted the palate must be in order to genuinely find them attractive. But to help us along, manufacturers add salt to disguise or offset the sweetness, at levels that you would simply never add to home-cooked food.

Much of what lies in this chapter has fallen into the hands of large fast-food chains, and been corrupted in the process – be it fried chicken, burgers or kebabs. The homemade versions are delicious in their own right if completely different, and perfectly healthy, especially if you cut out the gratuitous carbs that tend to come with them and opt for some salad, or, at least a healthier take on the chips (see pages 148, 163 and 164).

As for the recipes that follow, don't frown too severely on fat. I find that sausages and mince marketed as having highly reduced levels of fat, five per cent for instance, don't cook up well. The mince is inherently tough, and sausages joyless. It is very much at the heart of this book to keep such considerations in perspective, hence the inclusion of recipes for cuts like pork shoulder, for lamb, for chicken WITH the skin, and so forth. Once you start stripping meat of every ounce of fat, then you start venturing into joyless diet territory. And, thankfully, fat is no longer considered to be the baddie it once was. So aim for a happy medium, ten per cent fat for mince should give you the succulence you are seeking without making for a greasy or unhealthy dish.

Classic hamburgers

There are very few of us who aren't enticed by the scent of a thick burger grilling over charcoal, the odd hiss as the juices drip onto the red-hot coals. And the best are no more than very good beef, chopped shallot, and some salt and pepper. If possible always try and buy your mince from a butcher who can tell you which cuts have gone into it, should you wish to know.

Given how well they freeze, I frequently make a double batch of these burgers so that, since they defrost in no time, they are at the ready for some easy suppers. Here lettuce leaves play the part of a bun, a quantum leap of imagination for some, but other classic garnishes are all present and correct, and it's easy enough to have some buns or pittas at the ready for those that want. Personally, I love the lettuce sandwich; a crisp green leaf is exactly what that juicy burger needs.

Serves 4

Burgers:
450g lean minced beef
1 tablespoon finely chopped
    shallots
sea salt, black pepper
8 small Romaine leaves, to serve

Garnishes:
English mustard
tomato ketchup
½ beefsteak tomato, core removed
    and sliced
½ red onion, peeled, halved and
    thinly sliced
8 cocktail gherkins, sliced

Mix together the mince, shallots and seasoning in a bowl. For an especially professional finish to your burgers, shape the mince, a quarter at a time, inside a 10cm pastry cutter with straight edges. Or, if you are happy with something more rustic, form the meat into balls using your hands, and then flatten these between your palms. Bear in mind that the burgers will shrink and fatten when you grill them. If you want you can make them in advance, then cover and chill them.

Either place a ridged cast-iron griddle or a large, dry frying pan over a medium–low heat, and cook the burgers for 4–5 minutes on each side. Place each burger within one of the lettuce leaves, smear over some mustard and then a little tomato ketchup. Next place a slice of tomato on top and season, then scatter over some sliced onion and gherkin, and close with a second leaf for eating in hand.

Carbohydrate 3.3g Protein 25.6g

Gratin of meatballs with plum tomatoes

Here meatballs are smothered in a chunky tomato sauce made with plum tomatoes. It makes for the easiest possible ragù as it's baked in the oven. If you like, you can add an egg to the meatball mixture, to help them hold together. Fresh oregano and marjoram can be used in lieu of thyme.

Now the trend for sliders – meatballs served in mini buns – has to catch on: baby burgers, what is there not to like? So you could also serve a supply of supple green leaves that can be rolled around a meatball and some of the sauce for eating in hand.

Serves 4

Meatballs:
extra virgin olive oil
1 onion, peeled and finely chopped
100g rindless unsmoked streaky
    bacon, finely diced
3 tablespoons fresh thyme leaves
700g lean minced beef
sea salt, black pepper

Tomato sauce:
1kg plum tomatoes
3 tablespoons tomato purée
2 garlic cloves, peeled and finely
    chopped
1 dried red chilli, finely chopped
freshly grated Parmesan to serve
    (optional)

For the meatballs, heat 2 tablespoons of olive oil in a large frying pan over a medium–low heat, add the onion and bacon and fry gently for about 5 minutes, stirring occasionally until soft and cooked through, adding 2 tablespoons of the thyme a couple of minutes before the end. Transfer the contents of the pan to a large bowl and leave to cool. Add the beef and some seasoning to the bowl and work together using a spoon. Shape the mixture into balls the size of a large walnut and set aside on a couple of plates.

To make the tomato sauce, bring a large pan of water to the boil and cut out a small cone from the top of each tomato to remove the core. Plunge the tomatoes into the boiling water for 20 seconds and then into a sink of cold water. Remove them and slip off the skins, halve and chop them. Place the tomatoes in a bowl and combine with the tomato purée, a tablespoon of olive oil, the garlic, chilli and some seasoning. Both the sauce and meatballs can be made in advance, in which case cover and chill them.

Heat a large, non-stick frying pan over a medium heat, add half the meatballs and colour them on all sides. Transfer them to a shallow ovenproof or gratin dish that holds them in a single layer with a little space between each one. Scrape the pan clean of any fat and chopped onion, and cook the remainder in the same fashion. Spoon the sauce over and between the meatballs.

Preheat the oven to 180°C fan/200°C electric/gas 6. Scatter over the remaining thyme, and drizzle another tablespoon of olive oil over the meatballs and bake for 40–45 minutes until the tomatoes on the top have started to singe at the tips. Serve with a bowl of Parmesan on the table to scatter over if wished.
Carbohydrate 13g Protein 45.3g

WITH BASIL PURÉE
You can also serve these with a drizzle of basil purée, made by whizzing 50g **basil leaves** and a small peeled **garlic clove** in a food processor until finely chopped, then gradually add 4 tablespoons of **extra virgin olive oil** and season to taste with **sea salt** and a squeeze of **lemon juice**.
Carbohydrate 13.8g Protein 45.8g

Middle Eastern lamb burgers

The four spices cumin, coriander, cinnamon and allspice capture the scent of the Middle East; an unlikely quartet, as individually they have such different characters, but together they make a charming mismatch. With fresh coriander, parsley and some olives, these are jazzier than the previous Classic hamburgers (page 66). And you still get to eat them between lettuce leaves.

Serves 4

Burgers:
450g lean minced lamb
1 tablespoon finely chopped shallots
2 garlic cloves, peeled and finely
    chopped
2 teaspoons ground cumin
1 teaspoon ground coriander
1 teaspoon ground cinnamon
¼ teaspoon ground allspice
sea salt, black pepper
8 small Romaine leaves, to serve

Garnishes:
1 beefsteak tomato, core removed
    and sliced
1 large handful of coriander sprigs
1 large handful of flat-leaf parsley
    sprigs
50g black olives, pitted and halved
a squeeze of lemon juice

Blend together the mince, shallots, garlic, spices and seasoning in a bowl. For an especially professional finish to your burgers, shape the mince a quarter at a time inside a 10cm pastry cutter with straight edges. Or, if you are happy with something more rustic, form the meat into balls using your hands, and then flatten these between your palms. Bear in mind that the burgers will shrink and fatten when you grill them. If you want you can make them in advance, then cover and chill them.

Either place a ridged cast-iron griddle over a medium–low heat or preheat a conventional grill to high, and cook the burgers for 4–5 minutes each side. Place each burger within one of the lettuce leaves, place a slice of tomato on top, then some herb sprigs and olives, and squeeze over a little lemon juice, and close with a second leaf for eating in hand.
Carbohydrate 4g Protein 22.5g

BARBECUED
Burgers are always great barbecued, in which case cook them over hot coals for 15–20 minutes in total. If you press down on them using a spatula you will also encourage the branding of stripes.

A trio of ragùs

Each of these has a different cultural identity, but they are all similar in style and adaptability. I am happy to eat them with a big salad, or with some roasted veg – peppers, aubergines and courgettes are all lovely (see pages 166–169). But it's easy enough to cook pasta, rice, tortillas or whatever others might fancy. Ideally use minced beef with about 10 per cent fat, and if it also announces its pedigree then so much the better. Equally, buy the best minced lamb on offer or visit the butcher.

SPAG BOL

This suppertime staple gets wheeled out in our house with embarrassing regularity. And no matter how much I cook it never goes to waste. Not so long ago we were having a Christmas drinks party, and my husband was concerned about providing for the possibility of any stragglers, which he numbered at a possible thirty, while I felt this was highly unlikely. But, once the seed of doubt had been sown, it remained a niggling worry. So, we agreed that I would cater for the drinks eats, and he would take care of anything required afterwards. He opted for Spag Bol.

Serves 6

25g unsalted butter
1 tablespoon extra virgin olive oil
1 onion, peeled and finely chopped
2 slim carrots, trimmed, peeled and thinly sliced
1 stick of celery, thinly sliced
2 tablespoons fresh oregano or marjoram leaves, or 1 teaspoon dried
4 garlic cloves, peeled and finely chopped
800g lean minced beef
150ml red wine
1 x 400g can chopped tomatoes
1 tablespoon tomato purée
150ml chicken or beef stock
1 small dried red chilli, crumbled
sea salt, black pepper
3 tablespoons freshly grated Parmesan, plus extra to serve (optional)
freshly grated nutmeg

Heat the butter and the olive oil in a medium saucepan over a medium heat, and fry the onion, carrots, celery and fresh oregano or marjoram for about 10 minutes, stirring frequently, until softened and glossy, adding the garlic just before the end. Add the mince, turn up the heat and fry, stirring frequently, until the meat changes colour. Add the wine, tomatoes, purée, stock, chilli, and oregano if using dried, and season with a little salt. Bring to the boil, then simmer over a low heat for 1 hour, stirring now and again. There should still be enough juices at the end to moisten a pile of spaghetti (should that be the call), so if necessary cover it towards the end. Skim off any excess fat, stir in 3 tablespoons of Parmesan if including, and season with nutmeg. Serve the Bolognese sauce with a shower of Parmesan if wished and a grinding of black pepper.
Carbohydrate 6.1g Protein 28g

CHEAT'S SPAG BOL

Here a jar of good ragù will provide the character normally built in by chopped veggies and a can of tomatoes. Go for an established Italian name such as Bertolli or Sacla, both of them old hands who know what they're doing.

Serves 6

Gently fry 1 finely chopped **onion** in 2 tablespoons of **extra virgin olive oil** in a medium saucepan for about 5 minutes until softened and lightly coloured. Add 800g lean **minced beef**, turn up the heat and continue to fry until the meat changes colour, stirring occasionally. Add 1 tablespoon of **fresh thyme leaves**, 350–400g jar of **ragù**, 150ml **white wine**, 150ml **chicken** or **beef stock**, and some **sea salt**. Bring to the boil and simmer for 1 hour. Season with **nutmeg**.
Carbohydrate 7.3g Protein 27.8g

CHILLI CON CARNE

A hint of chilli and spices, fab with Guacamole (see page 202) and a tomato salad. Or you could scoop this up with small, crisp lettuce leaves, with the usual asides like pickled chillies and sour cream.

Serves 6

1 onion, peeled and cut into pieces
2 slim carrots, trimmed, peeled and
   chopped
1 stick of celery, chopped
25g unsalted butter
1 tablespoon extra virgin olive oil
1 tablespoon finely chopped or
   sliced medium-hot red chilli
2 tablespoons fresh oregano or
   marjoram leaves, or 1 teaspoon
   dried
4 garlic cloves, peeled and finely
   chopped
1 heaped teaspoon ground cumin
800g lean minced beef
150ml red wine
1 x 400g can chopped tomatoes
1 tablespoon tomato purée
150ml chicken or beef stock
sea salt
a couple of handfuls of coarsely
   chopped fresh coriander, plus
   extra to serve
black pepper

Put the onion, carrot and celery in the bowl of a food processor and whizz until finely chopped. Heat the butter and the olive oil in a medium saucepan over a medium heat, and fry the vegetable mixture with the chilli and fresh oregano or marjoram for about 10 minutes until softened and glossy, stirring frequently and adding the garlic and cumin just before the end.

Add the minced beef, turn up the heat and fry, stirring frequently, until the meat changes colour. Add the wine, tomatoes, purée, stock, and oregano if using dried, and season with salt. Bring to the boil, then simmer over a low heat for 1 hour, stirring now and again. The juices should be rich and well reduced. Skim off any excess fat, stir in the coriander and taste for seasoning. Serve with extra coriander scattered over.
Carbohydrate 6.3g Protein 31.2g

HERBY LAMB RAGÙ

I love the liveliness of this ragù with its spices, herbs and orange juice, leaning towards the East of the Med.

Serves 6

3 tablespoons extra virgin olive oil
4 shallots, peeled and finely
    chopped
3 garlic cloves, peeled and finely
    chopped
1/3 teaspoon ground allspice
1/3 teaspoon ground cinnamon
1kg lean minced lamb
400ml smooth fresh orange juice
2 heaped tablespoons tomato purée
sea salt
cayenne pepper
2 bunches of spring onions (8–10
    in each), trimmed and sliced
1 handful of coarsely chopped
    coriander
1 handful of coarsely chopped
    flat-leaf parsley

Heat 2 tablespoons of olive oil in a medium-large saucepan over a medium heat and fry the shallots for a minute or so until softened and translucent, stirring frequently, then stir in the garlic and spices and fry for a further minute. Add the mince, turn up the heat and fry until the meat changes colour. Add the orange juice, the tomato purée, some salt and a little cayenne pepper, bring to the boil, then cover and cook over a low heat for 1 hour.

Leave the ragù to stand for 5 minutes. Heat a large frying pan over a high heat, toss the spring onions with the remaining tablespoon of oil and fry for several minutes until softened and golden, stirring frequently – they will reduce considerably during the frying. Skim any excess fat off the ragù juices, stir in the herbs, transfer the ragù to a warm gratin or shallow serving dish and scatter over the spring onions.

Carbohydrate 8.7g Protein 35.4g

Jerk chicken

Seasoned Pioneers make a fab Caribbean jerk mix, deliciously heady with allspice, thyme, cayenne, nutmeg and cloves (see page 14). Blend it with lemon, garlic and olive oil and you have an instant marinade. 'Mini' chicken fillets, which are basically the small fillet that runs below the main fillet, are great here as they cook through in minutes, and being slim they turn nicely feisty by absorbing lots of the marinade. Guacamole is good here (see page 202), and a tomato salad. As are little pittas or tacos if you're catering for teenagers too.

Serves 6

Marinade:
2 tablespoons lemon juice
3 tablespoons extra virgin olive oil
1 garlic clove, peeled and crushed
  to a paste
2 teaspoons jerk seasoning

Chicken:
800g mini free-range chicken
  fillets
sea salt

Up to a couple of hours in advance of eating, combine all the marinade ingredients in a bowl or airtight plastic container. Carefully slice either side of the white tendon if it is present in the fillets, and remove it. Add the chicken to the marinade and coat it. Cover and chill if not cooking straight away.

Heat a large, non-stick frying pan over a medium heat, season the chicken fillets with salt and fry in batches for a couple of minutes on each side, until golden and firm when pressed.
Carbohydrate 0.7g Protein 32.1g

Marinated chicken thighs

I'm a huge fan of chicken thighs, which combine everything that's good about the breast, with the succulence and added flavour of the dark meat. They're streets ahead of drumsticks, but when they cook bone-in they also have the same advantages. So these make for great snacking.

Serves 4

Marinade:
juice of 1 lemon
4 tablespoons extra virgin olive oil
3 garlic cloves, peeled and crushed
to a paste
1 teaspoon paprika

Chicken:
8 free-range chicken thighs
sea salt, black pepper

Whisk all the marinade ingredients together in a large bowl or airtight plastic container. Add the chicken thighs, and coat thoroughly with the marinade. Cover and leave in the fridge for a couple of hours or overnight, turning them once.

Preheat the oven to 200°C fan/220°C electric/gas 7 and line the base of a grill pan with foil. Season the thighs on both sides and lay them on a rack inside the grill pan. Spoon over a little of the marinade and cook for 30–35 minutes until the outside is golden and the flesh comes away from the bone with ease. These can be eaten hot or cold.
Carbohydrate 0.7g Protein 40.5g

BARBECUED
Season the chicken thighs on both sides and barbecue for 30–50 minutes in total, turning them as necessary, and starting them off well away from the coals to ensure they cook through without burning.

Sausage and onion roast

The majority of French sausages, or *saucisses*, are made with 100 per cent meat, give or take the spices, onion and other flavourings, but certainly with no rusk or bread. Increasingly, UK producers are starting to follow suit, given the demand for gluten-free bangers and also ones without any carbs, so it is now possible to buy a good selection in most supermarkets. A pot of buttery mash is as welcome as ever, such as the Spring root mash (see page 162).

Serves 6

5 tablespoons extra virgin olive oil
1.2kg pork sausages
6 red onions, peeled, halved and
    sliced
6 leeks, trimmed and thickly sliced
a small bunch of thyme (about
    15 sprigs)
sea salt, black pepper

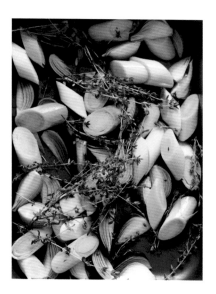

Heat a tablespoon of oil in a large frying pan over a medium heat and colour the sausages on both sides, in two batches if you need to, then transfer them to a large bowl. Arrange the onions, leeks and thyme sprigs on the base of one or two roasting pans (I use a 25 x 38cm pan, and a smaller 20 x 30cm pan) – the vegetables need to be about 2.5cm deep. Drizzle over the remaining oil and season, then arrange the sausages on top, spaced about 5cm apart.

Preheat the oven to 170°C fan/190°C electric/gas 5 and roast the sausages and vegetables for 1 hour, stirring every 20 minutes until the vegetables are silky and coloured; they will reduce considerably in the process of cooking. Discard the thyme sprigs as you serve the sausages with the vegetables.
Carbohydrate 13.2g Protein 51g

WITH MUSTARD SAUCE

For a creamy mustard sauce to go with the sausages, while they are roasting, blend 225ml **sour cream** with 1½ tablespoons of **Dijon mustard** in a bowl (this can be done well in advance). You could also scatter over some coarsely chopped **flat-leaf parsley**.
Carbohydrate 15g Protein 52.4g

Aubergine-wrapped Greek sausages with roast tomatoes

This is about as close as you are going to get to a sausage roll in this book, so bend your imagination to a heart of sausage encased in a succulent aubergine wrap. For a full-on Greek spread you could dish this up with toasted haloumi and a big salad of Cos leaves, some Tzatziki too, perhaps (see page 81).

Serves 4

600g lean minced lamb
1 shallot, peeled and finely chopped
1 garlic clove, peeled and crushed
    to a paste
1 teaspoon ground cumin
¼ teaspoon dried chilli flakes
sea salt, black pepper
2 good-sized aubergines, ends
    removed
extra virgin olive oil
500g mixed red and yellow cherry
    and cocktail tomatoes, halved
4 tablespoons oregano leaves

To make the sausages, blend the minced lamb, shallot, garlic, cumin, chilli and a little salt in a bowl. Taking a heaped tablespoon of the mixture at a time, form into 12 spindle-shaped sausages 8–9 cm long. Heat a large, non-stick frying pan over a high heat and colour these all over, then set aside. You will probably need to do this in two batches.

Preheat the oven to 200°C fan oven/220°C electric/gas 7. Slice off the outer edge of each aubergine lengthways and reserve these outer slices for another use. Then thinly slice each aubergine lengthways to give you 6 slices (12 in all). Heat a clean large, non-stick frying pan over a high heat, brush as many aubergine slices as will fit in a single layer with oil on one side, and season. Fry oiled-side down for 1½–2 minutes, then brush the top side with oil and fry likewise. They don't need to be fully cooked through, just coloured. Remove to a plate and cook the remainder in the same fashion.

Starting at the rounded end of each aubergine slice, roll up a sausage, skewer with a cocktail stick and arrange in a large roasting dish (about 25 x 38cm) with a little space between. Toss the tomatoes with half of the oregano, some seasoning and a couple of tablespoons of oil and scatter over and between the rolls. Scatter over the remaining oregano, drizzle over a little more oil and bake for 30–35 minutes until everything is nice and golden.
Carbohydrate 8.9g Protein 31.7g

A kebab or two

Here are a couple of very easy kebabs that are particularly good for a barbecue, both of which are delicious served with Tzatziki (see page 81), or the AKA potato salad (see page 202). For a hand-held kebab, slip the lamb or chicken pieces off the skewer onto a large Romaine leaf and slather with the Tzatziki. Some Crispy roast onions (see page 166) are also very welcome.

LOULOU KEBABS
These are like spicy hamburgers on sticks, and a great favourite in our house.

Makes 8

700g lean minced lamb
1 shallot, peeled and finely chopped
2 tablespoons finely chopped
    flat-leaf parsley
½ teaspoon each ground cumin,
    cinnamon and nutmeg
sea salt, black pepper

Combine all the ingredients for the kebabs with 1½ teaspoons of salt and some black pepper using your hands, then divide the mixture into 8 balls the size of a small apple. Shape each one of these into a long, flat sausage 10–12cm in length and about 3cm wide and slip a skewer lengthways through the middle so the tip is just concealed by the end of the kebab. Set these aside on a plate – they can be made up to 24 hours in advance, in which case cover and chill them.

Place a ridged cast-iron griddle over a medium–high heat and grill the kebabs for about 15 minutes in all, cooking them on all 4 sides. You may need to cook them in batches. Accompany with Tzatziki (see page 81).
Carbohydrate 0.5g Protein 16.4g

BARBECUE
Barbecue the kebabs for 15–20 minutes in total, turning them as necessary and cooking them on all 4 sides.

PAPRIKA CHICKEN KEBABS

While pieces of vegetable between morsels of chicken on a kebab always look colourful, they never grill up very well. I prefer a skewer crammed with chicken cheek to cheek, and to roast some onions separately for throwing over at the end (see page 166).

Makes 6

Marinade:
juice of 1 lemon
4 tablespoons extra virgin olive oil
3 garlic cloves, peeled and crushed
    to a paste
2 teaspoons paprika
1 tablespoon fresh thyme leaves

Chicken:
6 skinless free-range chicken
    breasts
sea salt, black pepper

Whisk together all the ingredients for the marinade in a large bowl or airtight plastic container. Remove the white tendon beneath each chicken breast, then cut them into hearty cubes, about 5cm, add to the bowl and coat thoroughly with the marinade. Cover and leave in the fridge for a couple of hours or overnight. Season the chicken and thread onto 20cm skewers (see below).

Place a ridged cast-iron griddle (ideally a double one) over a medium heat and grill the kebabs on all 4 sides for 15–20 minutes in total. You may need to cook them in batches.
Carbohydrate 1.1g Protein 35.2g

BARBECUE
Season the chicken kebabs and barbecue for 20–25 minutes in total, turning them as necessary, and starting them off well away from the coals to ensure they cook through without burning.

TZATZIKI

This makes a sizeable quantity, but my children adore it and we seem to get through it by the bucketload. It's great with both the chicken, and the Loulou kebabs on the previous page.

Serves 6

500g zero-fat Greek yogurt
extra virgin olive oil
2 teaspoons lemon juice
1 garlic clove, peeled and crushed
    to a paste
4 tablespoons finely sliced mint
a pinch of sugar
sea salt, black pepper
2 cucumbers

Blend the yogurt with 2 tablespoons of olive oil, the lemon juice, garlic, mint, sugar and a little seasoning in a bowl. Peel the cucumbers, slit them in half lengthways and scoop out the seeds using a teaspoon. Now thinly slice them into half moons and stir these into the yogurt mixture. Check the seasoning, then pile it into a clean bowl and pour over a little olive oil. This can be made up to a couple of hours in advance, in which case cover and set aside somewhere cool.
Carbohydrate 5.1g Protein 9.1g

TIP: Bamboo skewers are prettier than metal ones, which can look a little fierce on the plate. They can be found in most Oriental delis and come in different lengths. To prevent them from scorching, soak them in water before assembling the kebabs.

*But if you are using **metal skewers**, you will find that flat rather than round ones prevent the meat from slipping when you turn them.*

Spicy ribs

Barbecue marinades tend to be loaded with sugar or honey, which aids their caramelisation. But I find you get equally golden ribs with this marinade, and the vinegar brings out the flavour of the pork. While ribs tend to be a fatty cut, it is this layering that allows them to slow-roast to such tender succulent results, and most of it renders in the throes of cooking and is drained off in any case. My preference is for St Louis ribs, these are cut from the belly and that much meatier than back ribs; you may also encounter 'belly ribs', which are one and the same without the rind. A crisp green salad and, as ever, it's fingers in.

Serves 6

Marinade:
4 tablespoons tomato ketchup
4 tablespoons groundnut oil
1 tablespoon English mustard
2 tablespoons Worcestershire sauce
2 tablespoons dry sherry or
    Madeira
1 tablespoon red wine vinegar
4 garlic cloves, peeled and crushed
    to a paste
2 teaspoons finely grated fresh ginger
1 heaped teaspoon garam masala

Ribs:
2kg free-range St Louis pork ribs
sea salt
a handful of medium-hot red
    chillies (optional)

Whisk together all the ingredients for the marinade in a large bowl. Add the pork ribs, turning to coat them in the mixture. Cover and chill for at least 1 hour, ideally several. You can also marinate them overnight.

Preheat the oven to 160°C fan/180°C electric/gas 4. Turn the ribs to coat them in the marinade and arrange in two roasting trays in a single layer spaced slightly apart, seasoning them on both sides with salt. Tuck in the chillies if using. Cover with foil and roast for 1 hour. Uncover the ribs and coat with any residual marinade, there should be some juices in the base of the pan, and roast for a further 45 minutes or until golden and the juices have reduced to a sticky residue. Serve 15–20 minutes out of the oven once they are cool enough to handle, with chillies for those who wish to brave them.
Carbohydrate 4.4g Protein 31.9g

PIES & CASSEROLES

Pies are conceivably one of the trickiest of our favourite dishes to find a way round. Ultimately they are a casserole or stew, encased in carbs by the way of potatoes or pastry. But this can just as readily be a vegetable layer on top, and if the match is right this is no trading down. When it contributes to the ensemble and is in keeping with the filling – some crispy onions with beef, celeriac with lamb, courgettes with salmon, the vegetables will double up as an aside. Which is not to stop you dishing up a big bowl of vegetable mash.

Casseroles too are all the better for being kept in the comfort zone. It is the juices or copious gravy that demands something to mop it up, and even though that might traditionally take the form of rice, pasta, potatoes or polenta, a vegetable purée can be equally alluring, and you have the added advantage of being able to marry it to suit.

Cottage pie with leek and cauliflower mash

This delicate pale green mash has that wholesome silky texture that is exclusive to leek soups and purées. Smothered with cherry tomatoes and spring onions before being baked the pie is every bit as lavish as the original. Don't worry too much about the ratio of leeks to cauli – you want more or less 1.2kg in total but it doesn't matter too much how you weight them.

Serves 6

Mince:
50g unsalted butter
3 tablespoons extra virgin olive oil
2 slim carrots, trimmed, peeled and
    thinly sliced
2 sticks celery heart, trimmed and
    thinly sliced
1 onion, peeled and finely chopped
2 tablespoons fresh oregano or
    marjoram leaves, or 1
    tablespoon fresh thyme leaves
1kg lean minced beef
200ml red wine
1 x 400g can chopped tomatoes
2 tablespoons tomato purée
2 teaspoons Worcestershire sauce
sea salt, black pepper

Mash:
600g leeks (trimmed weight),
    thickly sliced
600g small cauliflower florets
freshly grated nutmeg
a bunch of slim spring onions
    (about 75g trimmed weight),
    sliced
150g small cherry tomatoes, halved

Heat half the butter and a tablespoon of olive oil in a medium saucepan over a medium heat, add the sliced and chopped vegetables and herbs, and fry for 5–8 minutes, stirring occasionally, until softened and lightly coloured. Add the meat, turn up the heat and cook, stirring occasionally, until it changes colour. Add the red wine, chopped tomatoes and purée, Worcestershire sauce and some seasoning. Bring to a simmer then cook over a very low heat for 50–60 minutes, stirring occasionally, until nearly all the juices have been absorbed. Keep a careful eye on it towards the end to prevent it from burning. Tilt the pan and skim off any surface fat, then taste for seasoning.

While the mince cooks, start making the mash. Place the leeks and cauliflower in a large saucepan with 150ml water, dot with the remaining 25g butter, add a tablespoon of olive oil and some salt. Bring the liquid to a simmer, then cover and cook over a low heat for 15–25 minutes, stirring halfway through, until very tender. Tip the contents of the pan into a food processor and reduce to a purée, seasoning it with nutmeg and more salt if necessary. You tend to get the best results if you do this in a couple of batches.

Transfer the mince to a shallow ovenproof dish or roasting tin (about 20 x 30cm), pressing down to level the surface. Spread the mash on top. You can make the pie in advance, in which case leave to cool, cover and chill.

Preheat the oven to 180°C fan/200°C electric/gas 6. Toss the spring onions and cherry tomatoes with the remaining tablespoon of oil and scatter over the surface. Bake for 40–45 minutes until the vegetables on top are golden.
Carbohydrate 13.3g Protein 43.8g

Celeriac cottage pie

Another cottage pie, but here the usual mash is replaced with a celeriac purée. This vegetable has a particular affinity with beef, somehow they seek to outdo each other's bass notes. This pie is altogether more rugged that the preceding one, which only emphasises further how different vegetables can shape the character of a dish in a way that starchy carbs can't.

Serves 6

Mince:
1 carrot, trimmed, peeled and cut up
1 celery stick, cut up
1 onion, peeled and cut up
2 tablespoons extra virgin olive oil
2 teaspoons fresh thyme leaves
900g lean minced beef
300ml red wine
2 tablespoons tomato purée
150ml beef or chicken stock
sea salt, black pepper

Mash:
a slug of vinegar, (white wine or cider)
1.5 kg celeriac, skin cut off, and cut into chunks
100g unsalted butter
freshly grated nutmeg
milk
2 medium egg yolks

Whizz the carrot, celery and onion in a food processor to finely chop them. Heat the oil in a medium saucepan over a medium heat, add the chopped vegetables and thyme and fry for about 5 minutes, stirring occasionally, until softened. Add the minced beef, turn up the heat to high and continue to fry, stirring frequently, until it changes colour. Add the wine and simmer until well reduced, then stir in the tomato purée, the stock and some seasoning, bring to the boil and simmer over a low heat for 30 minutes. Spoon off any excess fat from the surface.

While the meat is cooking, bring a large saucepan of water to the boil and acidulate it with a slug of vinegar. Add the celeriac and simmer for 20–30 minutes until tender, then drain into a colander and leave for a few minutes for the surface moisture to evaporate.

Place the celeriac with the butter and some salt, pepper and nutmeg in a liquidiser, and purée, adding a drop of milk to kickstart the process. You'll probably need to do this in batches, transferring it to a bowl as you go. Stir in the egg yolks.

Transfer the mince to a shallow ovenproof dish or roasting tin (about 20 x 30cm), pressing down to level the surface. Spread the celeriac on top. You can make the pie in advance, in which case leave to cool, then cover and chill.

Preheat the oven to 190°C fan/210°C electric/gas 7 and bake for 35–40 minutes.
Carbohydrate 10g Protein 38.5g

Autumn veggie lasagne

The creation of this lasagne was inspired by the French tradition of stuffed cabbage, which is one of the Gallic definitions of comfort, and truly delicious when carefully prepared, but a step too fiddly in my book. So this sets out to steal the spirit for an Italian great, by layering a richly flavoured ragù with tender spring greens and sautéed mushrooms. A Celeriac or Cauliflower mash would both be lovely here (see pages 157 and 158).

Serves 6

Ragù:
4 tablespoons extra virgin olive oil
1 large onion, peeled and finely chopped
1 large carrot, peeled, halved lengthways and finely sliced
2 sticks celery, trimmed and finely sliced
75g diced rindless unsmoked back bacon
2 garlic cloves, peeled and finely chopped
1kg lean minced beef
300ml red wine
1 x 400g can chopped tomatoes
150ml chicken stock
3 tablespoons tomato purée
1 bay leaf
sea salt, black pepper

Vegetables:
200g young spring greens (trimmed weight)
400g chestnut mushrooms, stalks trimmed and sliced

Top:
2 heaped tablespoons crème fraîche
50g freshly grated Parmesan

To make the ragù, heat 2 tablespoons of olive oil in a large saucepan over a medium heat, add the onion, carrot, celery and bacon and fry for 8–10 minutes until aromatic and lightly coloured, stirring in the garlic just before the end. Add the mince and cook, stirring frequently until it seals and changes colour. Pour in the red wine and simmer until this is well-reduced. Add the canned tomatoes, chicken stock, tomato purée, bay leaf and a grinding of black pepper. Bring to a simmer, then cook over a low heat for 40–45 minutes until almost all the liquid has evaporated, keeping an eye on it, and stirring towards the end. Leave the sauce to stand for a few minutes, then skim off any oil on the surface. Taste for salt, depending on the saltiness of the bacon it may or may not require any extra. Discard the bay leaf.

While the ragù is simmering, bring a large saucepan of salted water to the boil, add the greens and blanch for 2 minutes, then drain into a colander. To cook the mushrooms, heat a tablespoon of oil in a large frying pan over a medium heat, add half the mushrooms, season and fry for about 5 minutes, stirring frequently, until softened and golden, and any liquid given out has evaporated. Transfer these to a bowl and cook the remainder in the same way.

Select a 20 x 30cm roasting tin or baking dish of an equivalent size, and layer the ingredients as follows. Cover the base of the dish with a third of the ragù, then cover with half the greens, scatter over half the mushrooms and repeat with the remaining ingredients, so that you end up with three layers of ragù and two of vegetables. If making the lasagne in advance, leave it to cool before dotting the crème fraîche over the top, and scattering with the Parmesan.

Preheat the oven to 180°C fan/200°C electric/gas 6 and bake the lasagne for 45 minutes or until golden and bubbling on the surface.
Carbohydrate 10.3g Protein 46.8g

Lancashire hotpot

Traditionally this is made using best end neck chops, but thick slices of neck fillet are equally good, or diced shoulder is always readily available. Celeriac takes the place of the usual slices of potato, turning deliciously tender underneath and crispy on top.

Serves 6

1 tablespoon groundnut or
    vegetable oil
50g unsalted butter
sea salt, black pepper
1.2 kg neck fillet or shoulder, cut
    into 5cm chunks, or 1.5 kg best
    end neck chops
2 onions, peeled, halved and thinly
    sliced
800g carrots, trimmed, peeled and
    cut diagonally into roughly 5cm
    lengths
1 bay leaf
2 teaspoons Worcestershire sauce
700g celeriac (skinned weight)

Preheat the oven to 170°C fan/190°C electric/gas 5. Heat the oil and half the butter in a large cast-iron casserole over a medium heat, season the meat and colour on all sides, working in batches so as not to overcrowd the casserole, removing it to a bowl as you go. Tip off the excess fat, leaving just a couple of tablespoons in the casserole. Add the onions and fry for several minutes until golden – keep a careful eye on the pan as this will happen quite quickly. Return the meat to the pan, add the carrots and the bay leaf and stir to mix everything together. Stir the Worcestershire sauce into 700ml water and pour this over, and add some seasoning.

Cut the celeriac downwards into four or eight wedges depending on its size, and thinly slice across, you can do this with the slicing attachment on a food processor. Level the lamb and carrots as far as possible (the liquid won't quite cover them), and bring to the boil. Layer the celeriac on top, seasoning the layers as you go, and dot with the remaining butter. Cover and cook in the oven for 1¼ hours, then uncover and cook for a further hour until the celeriac is golden and crisp. You can also pop the hotpot briefly under a hot grill if you want to colour the top further.
Carbohydrate 16.9g Protein 39.6g

Cheat's meatball moussaka

The cheat here is because the aubergine is roasted rather than grilled or fried, which also reduces the amount of fat it absorbs, the ragù is ready-made, and there is a speedy white sauce, which together make this one a cinch compared to the usual long-haul. I like to eat it scooped onto the small crisp leaves of a Cos heart; the process of getting in there with my fingers takes me closer to a Greek taverna than a knife and fork.

Serves 6

Aubergines:
2 aubergines, ends discarded,
    cut into 1cm slices
extra virgin olive oil
sea salt, black pepper

Meatballs:
800g lean minced lamb
1 heaped teaspoon dried oregano
½ teaspoon ground cinnamon
¼ teaspoon cayenne pepper
2 x 350g jars tomato ragù eg Sacla

Sauce:
500g zero-fat Greek yogurt
2 medium eggs, beaten
200g 'light' halloumi, grated
2 heaped tablespoons fresh oregano
    or marjoram leaves, or 1 heaped
    tablespoon lemon thyme leaves

Preheat the oven to 190°C fan/210°C electric/gas 7. Lay the aubergine slices out on a baking tray, brush both sides with oil, and season the top. Roast for 15 minutes, then turn the slices and cook for a further 10–15 minutes until golden.

In the meantime, mix together all the meatball ingredients except the ragù in a large bowl, seasoning the mixture with salt, then use your hands to roll it into balls the size of a walnut. Heat a large, non-stick frying pan over a medium–high heat and colour the meatballs, half at a time, on all sides, draining off any fat between batches, then transfer them to a bowl. Carefully mix in the ragù.

Arrange the meatballs in a 30cm/2-litre oval gratin dish or one of similar size, and lay the aubergine slices on top, overlapping as necessary. Whisk the yogurt with the eggs in a medium bowl, then stir in half the halloumi. Spread on top of the aubergine layer and scatter over the remaining cheese. Toss the herbs with a tablespoon of oil and scatter over the surface. Bake for 40–45 minutes until puffy and golden. Serve 10–20 minutes out of the oven or, on a fine day, it is also delicious eaten warm rather than hot, in the Greek spirit of things.
Carbohydrate 14.8g Protein 46.8g

Imam bayildi

These aubergines, with their tomato and herb filling, will stand in for pies for any vegetarians. So succulent, I'll run with the Imam fainting with pleasure on eating it rather than being shocked at the amount of oil, as the two contrasting legends about this dish go. I cannot imagine Turkish cooks divulged that kind of information to their great leaders; I should have thought they played their cards very close to their chest so as to remain indispensable.

Serves 4

2 aubergines, end of stalks trimmed
extra virgin olive oil
sea salt, black pepper
2 beefsteak tomatoes (about 250g each)
1 large onion, peeled, halved and thinly sliced
5 garlic cloves, peeled and finely chopped
3 tablespoons each coarsely chopped fresh flat-leaf parsley, dill and basil

Preheat the oven to 180°C fan/200°C electric/gas 6 and heat a ridged cast-iron griddle over a medium heat for several minutes. Halve the aubergines lengthways and brush them all over with oil. Season and grill the cut surface for about 5 minutes until golden, then lay the aubergine halves, cut-side up, in a roasting dish. You will probably need to grill them half at a time, depending on the size of your griddle.

In the meantime bring a small saucepan of water to the boil and cut out a cone to remove the core from each tomato. Plunge them into the boiling water for about 20 seconds and then into cold water. Slip off their skins and coarsely chop them. Combine in a bowl with the onion, garlic and herbs, add some seasoning and 6 tablespoons of olive oil and toss.

Pile the vegetable mixture on top of the aubergines and roast for 40–45 minutes until the vegetables are nicely golden. Leave to cool for at least 15 minutes, and either serve warm or at room temperature with more olive oil poured over if wished.
Carbohydrate 13g Protein 3.7g

WITH OLIVES
Scatter some pitted **black olives** over the aubergines before serving them.
Carbohydrate 13g Protein 3.9g

Chicken and spinach pie with pumpkin mash

Many of the richest pies rely on a béchamel or white sauce, gorgeous but also off-limits when you start to consider what goes into it. So, a replacement? It has to be white, thick and silky. I adore sauces that come with the word *soubise* attached, meaning based on onions, so this was the answer.

Serves 6

Chicken:
3–4 tablespoons extra virgin olive oil
sea salt, black pepper
about 1.6kg free-range chicken thighs and drumsticks
150ml white wine
250ml chicken stock or water
75g unsalted butter, plus a knob
700g large or white onions, peeled, halved and sliced
500g spinach, washed

Mash:
1.2 kg pumpkin flesh, cut into even-sized chunks
freshly grated nutmeg
3 tablespoons coarsely chopped flat-leaf parsley

Heat a tablespoon of olive oil in a large cast-iron casserole over a medium–high heat. Season the chicken pieces and colour on both sides, half at a time. Drain off the fat, return all the chicken to the pan, add the wine and simmer to reduce by half. Pour in the chicken stock or water. Bring to a simmer, cover and cook over a low heat for 30 minutes, stirring halfway through.

In the meantime, melt 50g butter in a large saucepan over a low heat. Add the onions, sprinkle over a teaspoon of salt and gently fry them for 30 minutes, stirring frequently to prevent them colouring. By the end they should be lusciously silky and soft. While they cook, place the spinach in a large saucepan with just the water that clings to the leaves, cover and cook over a low heat for about 10 minutes, stirring halfway through, until it wilts. Drain into a sieve, pressing out the excess liquid with the back of a spoon or a potato masher, and coarsely chop.

Remove the chicken pieces to a bowl and leave the juices to settle – the fat will rise to the top. Once cool enough to handle, remove and discard the skin and bones and coarsely shred the flesh. Skim the fat off the surface of the cooking juices, and place 150ml of these in a liquidiser with the onions and whizz to a purée. Combine the shredded chicken and the sauce in a large bowl, and stir in the spinach. Transfer to a roasting pan or ovenproof dish (about 20 x 30cm).

For the mash, either steam the pumpkin for 15–20 minutes until tender, or place it in a large saucepan with a couple of centimetres of water, bring to the boil, cover and cook for a similar time. Drain into a sieve and press out the excess liquid using a potato masher. Transfer it to a large bowl and coarsely mash using a fork. Dice and stir in the remaining 25g butter, 2 tablespoons of olive oil, some seasoning and nutmeg, then fold in the parsley. Smooth the mash over the chicken and spinach, forking the surface into rough peaks. You can make the pie in advance, in which case leave to cool, cover and chill.

Preheat the oven to 190°C fan/210°C electric/gas 7 and bake the pie for 45 minutes. Heat the grill, dot the pie with the knob of butter and pop underneath until golden at the tips.
Carbohydrate 16.5g Protein 28.3g

Pork and apple braise with a mushroom crust

You can almost hear the rustle of desiccated leaves being trodden underfoot, such is the sense of autumn this braise offers up with its apples and mushrooms. It should prove warming throughout the winter months whenever the weather is cold and you are after something truly hearty.

Serves 6

extra virgin olive oil
sea salt, black pepper
800–900g pork tenderloin or fillet, sliced into medallions 1–2cm thick
125g unsmoked lardons, or diced rindless streaky bacon
1 onion, peeled, quartered and thinly sliced
2 garlic cloves, peeled and finely sliced
150ml Madeira or medium-dry sherry
400ml chicken stock
1 eating apple, peeled, quartered, cored and diced
1 Bramley cooking apple (200–250g), peeled, quartered, cored and diced
400g chestnut mushrooms, stalks trimmed and thinly sliced
100g button mushrooms, stalks trimmed and halved
a handful of fresh sage leaves
sour cream to serve (optional)

Preheat the oven to 130°C fan/150°C electric/gas 2. Heat a tablespoon of oil in a large cast-iron casserole over a medium–high heat, lightly season the pork medallions (the bacon will do a lot of the work) and colour on both sides, just a few at a time so as not to overcrowd the pan, then transfer them to a bowl. You may need to add a drop more oil between batches. Turn the heat down to medium–low, add another tablespoon of oil to the pan and fry the lardons or bacon for about 5 minutes until lightly coloured, then add the onion and fry for a further 5 minutes, stirring frequently, until golden and syrupy, and adding the garlic just before the end.

Add the Madeira or sherry and stir to take up all the sticky residue on the base of the pan, then return the pork to the pan, pour over the stock, bring to the boil, cover and cook in the oven for 2 hours.

Turn up the oven temperature to 190°C fan/210°C electric/gas 7. Skim off any fat from the surface of the cooking juices, and stir the apple into the casserole. Toss the mushrooms with 2 tablespoons of oil in a large bowl, season and scatter over the top. Scatter over the sage leaves and drizzle over another couple of tablespoons of oil. Return to the oven, uncovered, for 40–45 minutes until the sage leaves are crisp and the mushrooms turn a light gold. Tilt the casserole to skim off any fat from the surface of the juices, and serve with a dollop of sour cream if wished.

Carbohydrate 9.6g Protein 36.5g

Red wine steak casserole with crispy onions

This is everything you dream of in a steak supper in casserole form. The beef is very slowly braised with red wine, juniper and lardons, until meltingly tender and sitting in a rich, dark gravy, then finished in a hot oven with a layer of red onions that turn silky soft with a crispy top. A Broccoli mash would be lovely here (see page 158), or Carrot and swede (see page 156).

Serves 6

Beef:
25g unsalted butter
100g unsmoked lardons, or diced
    rindless streaky bacon
sea salt, black pepper
1.2 kg braising beef (eg chuck or
    blade), cut into 3–4cm pieces
1 bay leaf
a few sprigs of fresh thyme
about 10 juniper berries, secured in
    a small square of muslin or
    empty tea-bag
600ml red wine
150ml beef stock
300g small turnips, trimmed,
    peeled, and halved (or quartered
    if larger than a walnut)

Top:
700g red onions, peeled, halved and
    thinly sliced
3 tablespoons groundnut oil

Preheat the oven to 130°C fan/150°C electric/gas 2. Melt the butter in a large cast-iron casserole over a medium heat and fry the lardons or bacon for about 5 minutes, stirring frequently until golden, then transfer to a bowl. Lightly season the beef and colour on all sides, in batches, in the residual fat, transferring to the bowl with the lardons or bacon when ready. If a lot of fat remains, pour this off before proceeding.

Return all the meat to the pan, add the herbs, juniper berries, wine and stock, and season with black pepper (the bacon will provide some salt so this is best adjusted at the end of cooking). Bring to a simmer, skim off any foam on the surface, then cover and cook in the oven for 2½ hours, giving it a stir halfway through. Discard the herbs and spice bag. You can make the casserole in advance to this point, in which case leave to cool, cover and chill.

Turn up the oven temperature to 180°C fan/200°C electric/gas 6. Skim off any fat from the surface of the sauce, and if necessary reheat on the hob. Stir the turnips into the casserole.

To make the topping, toss the onions with the oil in a large bowl, separating out the strands, and scatter over the top. Return to the oven, uncovered, for another 55–60 minutes until the onions are golden and crisp on top.
Carbohydrate 12.2g Protein 46.3g

Ossobuco

For all the cachet attached to the name, this is a stew, and no more complex than any other we are accustomed to making. But it does have the added allure of a final scattering of gremolata, which whisks it out of its somnambulistic state after a couple of hours of slow cooking and back into the real world.

An authentic *Ossobuco alla Milanese* would not contain tomatoes (despite my own partiality); if you are in any doubt about this then you should read Anna Del Conte's *Secrets from an Italian Kitchen*. Even though today they are frequently added, for Anna this is a travesty. In lieu of a saffron risotto you could flavour the Cauliflower mash (see page 158) with saffron. Roast carrots are lovely with it as well (see page 168).

The ideal here are thick slices of shin of veal that will allow you to tie them around to keep them in place, thin slices are also more likely to buckle when seared. So if at all possible specify this to a butcher when buying. Either way, avoid small sections which will be all bone and no meat.

Serves 6

1.2kg ossobuchi (ideally cut 3.5–5cm thick)
extra virgin olive oil
sea salt, black pepper
15g unsalted butter
1 onion, peeled, halved and thinly sliced
2 carrots, trimmed, peeled and sliced diagonally
1 celery heart, trimmed and sliced diagonally
2 garlic cloves, peeled and finely chopped
3 plum tomatoes, skinned and chopped
200ml white wine
300ml chicken stock
a pinch of dried chilli flakes

Gremolata:
3 tablespoons finely chopped flat-leaf parsley
1 garlic clove, peeled and finely chopped
finely grated zest of 1 lemon

Preheat the oven to 140°C fan/160°C electric/gas 3. Make a small nick in the skin surrounding the ossobuchi on either side – you will need a very sharp knife for this. If they are thick enough, then also tie a piece of string around each one. Heat a tablespoon of oil in a large frying pan over a medium–high heat. Season the slices of veal and colour them on both sides, turning them frequently. You will need to do this in batches, replenishing the oil as necessary.

At the same time, heat 2 tablespoons of oil and the butter in a large cast-iron casserole over a medium heat – choose one that will hold the pieces of veal as far as possible in a single layer. Add the onion, carrots, celery and garlic and fry for 8–10 minutes, stirring frequently, until the vegetables are glossy and softened, without colouring. Stir in the tomatoes and cook for a minute longer, pressing them down. Nestle the ossobuchi between the vegetables. Pour over the wine and stock, and season with salt and a pinch of chilli flakes. The tips of the shins may peek out at the top, but they should be more or less covered. Bring the liquid to the boil, then cover and cook in the oven for 2 hours. Check the meat halfway through and gently press down the pieces so they are evenly submerged. Avoid moving them around however, otherwise the marrow may slip out from the centre of the bone, and this is the great treat.

Combine the parsley, garlic and lemon zest for the gremolata and serve sprinkled over the ossobuchi.
Carbohydrate 7.2g Protein 27.5g

THICKENED JUICES
If you're not avoiding carbs, then you can also dip the pieces of meat into **flour** before frying them, which will thicken the sauce just slightly.

Braised oxtail and onions

Most butchers will be able to provide you with oxtail, though it's worth a phone call a couple of days in advance to make sure they set some aside. You need good-sized joints, the last few tapered sections of the tail are fine for stock, but don't have any meat on them to speak of. Equally, you could use any other cut of braising steak here, such as rib trim, a classic daube cut. In this case, you can reduce the cooking time to a couple of hours.

Serves 6

Marinade:
150ml Madeira or medium sherry
2 garlic cloves, peeled and crushed
    to a paste
a few sprigs of fresh thyme
1 bay leaf, torn into pieces
¼ teaspoon ground cinnamon
¼ teaspoon ground nutmeg

Oxtail:
2kg oxtail, separated into joints
extra virgin olive oil
sea salt, black pepper
600g onions, peeled, halved and
    sliced
1 bottle (75cl) red wine
300g small chestnut or button
    mushrooms, stalks trimmed

To serve:
4 tablespoons chopped flat-leaf
    parsley mixed with finely grated
    zest of 1 orange

It isn't essential to marinate the meat, but it does give the dish that extra something. Combine the marinade ingredients in a large bowl, add the meat and baste it, cover and chill for about 6 hours or overnight, basting it halfway through if you remember.

Remove the meat from the marinade, and drain it on a double thickness of kitchen paper. Heat a tablespoon of olive oil in a large frying pan over a highish heat, season and add half the meat and sear to colour it on all sides. Remove it and cook the remainder in the same way – there shouldn't be any need to add more oil.

Heat a couple of tablespoons of oil in a large cast-iron casserole over a medium–high heat, add the onions and cook for 10–15 minutes, stirring occasionally, until golden. Add the marinade, the wine, some seasoning and then the oxtail. Bring to the boil, cover and cook over a low heat for 2 hours, giving it a stir halfway through.

Heat another couple of tablespoons of oil in a large frying pan over a medium–high heat, add the mushrooms, season them and sauté for a few minutes until lightly coloured. Stir these into the casserole and simmer for a further hour until the meat is fork tender.

Transfer the meat and mushrooms to a bowl, and simmer the juices to reduce them by about a third, discarding the herbs. Return the meat and mushrooms to the gravy and serve. The casserole can also be made in advance, in which case leave to cool and then chill, and remove any fat from the surface before reheating. Serve scattered with the chopped parsley and orange.
Carbohydrate 10.5g Protein 27.9g

Goulash

I like to cook chuck steak as a single large joint (as well as diced), which is more in keeping with the casserole cuts that I find in France where the pieces are cut larger and cook to the point where the meat pulls apart with a fork, rendering lovely long, succulent strands. The fact that it doesn't come pre-packed in the supermarket doesn't make this insurmountable, every butcher worthy of their striped apron will know what you are going on about.

Serves 6

Casserole:
extra virgin olive oil
sea salt, black pepper
1 x 1.2kg chuck steak in one piece
2 onions, peeled, halved and thinly
    sliced
2 green peppers, cored, deseeded
    and cut into thin strips
2 red peppers, cored, deseeded and
    cut into thin strips
2 teaspoons sweet paprika (mild)
1 teaspoon caraway seeds
1 x 400g can chopped tomatoes
200ml red wine
200ml beef stock

To serve:
sour cream and coarsely chopped
    flat-leaf parsley

Preheat the oven to 140°C fan/160°C electric/gas 3. Heat a tablespoon of oil in a large cast-iron casserole over a medium–high heat, season and sear the joint on all sides to colour it. Remove and turn the heat down a little, add another couple of tablespoons of oil to the pan and fry the onions for several minutes, stirring frequently, until starting to colour, then add the peppers and fry for a few minutes longer.

Stir in the paprika and the caraway seeds, then add the tomatoes, the wine, beef stock and some salt and bring to the boil. Nestle the joint between the vegetables, cover and cook in the oven for 3½ hours, turning the beef halfway through, by which time it should be meltingly tender. Taste for seasoning, and serve with a dollop of sour cream and lots of chopped parsley.
Carbohydrate 10.6g Protein 44.6g

ultimate Coq au vin

This classic casserole with its rich red wine gravy, button mushrooms and baby onions is one by which we judge many others. My treasured copy of Len Deighton's *Où est Le Garlic* seems to have gone missing, but I am quite sure that it must be in it. If you grew up at the end of the twentieth century without this dish being a fixture on the dinner table, you were deprived.

The ideal here is a whole chicken that has been cut into about eight pieces, but failing a dab hand with a pair of poultry shears, a mixture of thighs and drumsticks will do nicely. Mash turns this into the ultimately comforting line-up. The red wine needn't be anything special: cheap, cheerful and with plenty of character.

This is a casserole that reheats well, with the added advantage if you allow it to cool completely that you can remove any fat that has risen and set on the surface.

Serves 4

1 tablespoon vegetable oil
sea salt, black pepper
1.6 kg free-range chicken, jointed
    into 6–8 pieces, or a mixture of
    thighs and drumsticks
75g diced rindless unsmoked
    streaky bacon, or lardons
600ml red wine
150ml chicken stock
1 bay leaf
2 sprigs of fresh thyme
15g unsalted butter
200g baby onions or small shallots,
    peeled
100g button mushrooms, stalks
    trimmed if necessary
coarsely chopped flat-leaf parsley
    to serve

Preheat the oven to 130°C fan/150°C electric/gas 2. Heat the oil over a medium–high heat in a large cast-iron casserole. Season the chicken pieces and colour on both sides, in batches. Remove them to a bowl and pour off the fat, add the bacon or lardons and fry until they just begin to colour. Pour off all but a tablespoon of the fat. Return the chicken to the casserole. Pour in the red wine and chicken stock, and add the bay leaf and thyme. Heat the liquid until it just begins to bubble, then cover the casserole with a lid and cook in the oven for 1½ hours until the chicken is tender, turning the pieces on top halfway through. You can prepare the casserole to this point in advance, in which case leave to cool, cover and chill.

Either on removing the casserole from the oven or just before serving it, melt the butter in a non-stick frying pan over a low heat. Cook the onions for 15 minutes, turning them frequently, adding the mushrooms 5–7 minutes before the end. They should all be lightly golden. In the meantime, transfer the chicken pieces to a large bowl, carefully skim off any fat floating on the surface of the casserole and reduce the sauce by half, continuing to skim off any fat that rises to the surface. Return the chicken to the sauce, cover and gently reheat on the hob if necessary. Add the onions and mushrooms, taste for seasoning and serve straight away on warm plates, sprinkled with parsley.
Carbohydrate 2.6g Protein 56.1g

THICKENED JUICES
If you want to thicken the sauce slightly, then having returned the chicken to the casserole, sprinkle over 1 heaped tablespoon **flour** and cook, turning the pieces, for about 1 minute.
Carbohydrate 5.7g Protein 56.5g

Slow-roast pork shoulder with rosemary and anchovies

Slowly braised shoulder of pork is a great pot-roast, and I often opt for this over a classic roast as it guarantees to be tender and succulent, and I adore that 'pulled', falling-apart texture. Roasting pork joints can be hit and miss however carefully you approach the time and temperature.

But there is no need to do without the crackling. Ask your butcher (or beg, it's a bit of a chore) to slice off the rind, so the fat is evenly distributed between meat and skin, and to score it and then to re-tie the joint for you. You can then roast the rind separately, whacking up the oven temperature at the end to crisp it. Buttery spinach would be a good choice of veg with this and as ever some kind of mash, broccoli springs to mind.

Serves 6

⅓ teaspoon dried chilli flakes
2kg boned, rolled shoulder of pork, rind removed and scored
sea salt
1 tablespoon extra virgin olive oil
½ bottle of white wine
380ml chicken stock
4 salted anchovies, sliced
3 garlic cloves, peeled and smashed
3 sprigs of fresh rosemary, about 5cm long

Preheat the oven to 140°C fan/160°C electric/gas 3. Rub the chilli over the pork (don't worry about the ends) and very lightly season with salt. Heat the oil in a large frying pan over a medium–high heat and colour the pork all over, then transfer it to a large cast-iron casserole, placing it fat-side down. Add the wine, stock, anchovies, garlic and rosemary, bring to the boil, then cover and cook in the oven for 5 hours. Turn the pork halfway through, and at the same time rub some salt into the pork rind, put it skin-side up in a small roasting dish and then place in the oven.

Transfer the pork to a warm plate to rest for 20 minutes, loosely covering it with foil. In the meantime, turn up the oven temperature to 220°C fan/240°C electric/gas 8 to crisp the crackling for 10–15 minutes. You should see small bubbles appear below the surface.

Pour the juices into a jug, ideally transparent, and leave to stand for a minute or two for the oil to rise, then skim this off along with as many of the rosemary needles and sprigs as possible. Return the juices to the pan and simmer to reduce by about a third until well flavoured. The meat should be meltingly tender and pull apart with ease with a fork and spoon. Serve it with the juices and crackling.

Carbohydrate 2.8g Protein 62g

Guinea fowl braised with saffron and black olives

We don't have to save saffron and black olives for summer, they bring just as much sunshine in the midst of winter. But try to find a good-sized guinea fowl, in excess of 1.2kg, or buy two and freeze what you don't require for this recipe.

Serves 4

extra virgin olive oil
sea salt, black pepper
1 x 1.4kg guinea fowl, jointed
8 shallots, peeled
1 celery heart, trimmed and cut
    into 5cm lengths
150ml dry vermouth
1 x 400g can chopped tomatoes
100ml chicken stock
about 25 saffron filaments, ground
    and blended with 1 tablespoon
    boiling water
a pinch of dried chilli flakes
1 bay leaf
100g pitted green and black olives

Heat about a teaspoon of oil in a large frying pan over a medium heat, season the guinea fowl pieces and colour them on both sides, probably in batches. At the same time, heat a couple of tablespoons of oil in a large cast-iron casserole over a medium heat, add the shallots and celery and fry for 5–7 minutes, stirring occasionally, until glossy and lightly coloured. Add the guinea fowl pieces, the vermouth, tomatoes, stock, saffron, chilli, bay leaf and some salt. Give everything a good stir, arranging the guinea fowl pieces so as far as possible they are submerged. Bring the liquid to the boil, then cover and cook over a low heat for 1 hour, adding the olives halfway through.

The casserole can be prepared a day in advance, in which case leave to cool, cover and chill. To serve, skim off any fat on the surface, and reheat if necessary.
Carbohydrate 5.1g Protein 48.4g

Pot-roast rabbit with pastis

I tend to think of rabbit as a treat because we only rarely eat it in our house, most often when we are in France, where it is readily available, but a decent butcher should be able to provide the wherewithal. Rabbit makes for a fine lunch if you have friends round, a touch more sophisticated than chicken, though not dissimilar. It revels in mustard and other lively flavours – here pastis and lemon. You could also serve the sautéed liver scattered over some vegetables alongside, such as a root veg mash, or some cabbage.

Serves 4

2 tablespoons Dijon mustard
1 rabbit, jointed into 8 pieces,
    liver sliced and reserved
100g unsalted butter, clarified*
50g unsmoked lardons
450g baby leeks (trimmed weight),
    cut into 5cm lengths, or regular
    leeks sliced 1cm thick
1 bay leaf
2 sprigs of fresh thyme
150ml pastis, eg Ricard
juice of ½ lemon
100ml chicken stock or water
sea salt, black pepper
chopped dill fronds, to serve

Preheat the oven to 130°C fan/150°C electric/gas 2. Brush the mustard over the rabbit joints. Heat a large cast-iron casserole over a medium–high heat, add all but a tablespoon of the clarified butter, and colour the rabbit in batches, transferring the joints to a plate as they are ready. Add the lardons to the pan and fry for a few minutes, stirring occasionally, until they begin to colour.

Add the leeks to the pan with the herbs and continue to cook for about 7 minutes, stirring occasionally, until glossy and lightly coloured. Return the rabbit to the pan, pour over the pastis, lemon juice and stock or water. Lightly season (bearing in mind the bacon and mustard will do most of the work), then give everything a good stir, settling the rabbit pieces down as far as possible, though they won't be completely covered by the liquid. Cover and cook in the oven for 2 hours, turning the rabbit halfway through.

Transfer the cooked rabbit to a dish and simmer the juices vigorously for a few minutes to concentrate the flavours. Heat the reserved butter in a small frying pan over a high heat, add the liver and fry briefly until it changes colour and seems just firm, then season it. Return the rabbit to the sauce, and serve scattered with the liver and a little dill.
Carbohydrate 13.3g Protein 30.9g

---

*TIP: To clarify butter gently melt it then skim off the surface foam, decant and reserve the clear butter and discard the milky residue below.

THE CARVERY

Protein is the key to success in avoiding carbs. No other food type sustains you in the same way – you feel nourished, full but never overloaded or weighed down, and that satisfaction lasts for a long time. You don't get that rebound hunger as you do after a piece of fruit or a slice of toast or a muffin. In fact it's quite hard to eat too much, as you tend to stop when your body's had enough.

This chapter is a round-up of my stock favourite roasts, those that I turn to mid-week, and without fail at the weekend. Even if there are only two of us, it provides the wherewithal for grazing thereafter. A roast itself is the most basic of dishes – it's all the bits and bobs that go with it that constitute the hard work. Dressing a bird or joint for the oven usually takes around 5–10 minutes, so it's a good gain for minimal input. Another misconception is that roasts are very expensive whereas, aside from a treat such as a leg of lamb or joint of sirloin, most are considerably more affordable than a stack of ready-meals to feed the same number, or any other convenience food you are likely to buy on the hoof.

Rustic garlic roast chicken

Chicken roasted with garlic is a fab dish, but peeling all those heads is too fiddly to be bothering with on an average week-day, or weekend, and this rustic take where the bird is roasted surrounded by whole heads is just as good. With lemon, butter and thyme it is the perfect marriage of flavours.

This is one of the best cases for a crisp green salad, and if you forego a dressing you might just be able to justify drizzling the buttery juices from the roasting tin over the leaves.

Serves 4

**a bunch of fresh lemon thyme
    (about 20g)**
**1 x 1.6kg free-range chicken,
    untrussed**
sea salt, black pepper
4 heads of garlic, tops cut off
50g unsalted butter, melted
1 lemon, halved

Preheat the oven to 190°C fan/210°C electric/gas 7. Spread two-thirds of the thyme sprigs over the base of a roasting tin that will accommodate the chicken with a little room to spare around the sides, place the chicken on top and season it. Pull half the thyme leaves off the remaining sprigs and scatter over the chicken with the sprigs, then surround with the garlic heads. Drizzle the butter over the chicken and the garlic, squeeze over the lemon juice and pop the lemon halves inside the cavity of the bird. Roast for 50–55 minutes, basting the garlic halfway through.

Leave the chicken to rest in the tin for 15 minutes, then transfer both the chicken and the garlic to a warm plate, tipping any juices inside the bird back into the tin. Carve the chicken, adding any juices that have collected to the tin. Discard the thyme sprigs and rewarm the juices, skimming off the butter first if wished. Spoon the juices over the chicken accompanied by the garlic, squeezing it out of its casing as you eat.
Carbohydrate 3.7g Protein 52.2g

Serves 6

… OR GUINEA FOWL
For a slightly more special occasion or when you are feeding six people, then you could roast two **guinea fowl** (about 1.1kg each) with six **heads of garlic**. Space them slightly apart in a roasting tin, place ½ **lemon** inside each bird, and increase the **butter** to 75g and roast for 45–50 minutes then leave to rest as before.
Carbohydrate 5.8g Protein 58.5g

Lemon and spice roast chicken

This is one of my favourite methods for a simple week-day chicken, I endlessly play around with the spices, quite often it's za'atar or another Middle Eastern blend, maybe a curry powder, and the thyme is optional. So treat it as a blueprint.

I think this one is a lovely summery roast, even more so if you serve it with the fattoush. The chicken emerges with a deep golden skin, and the pan juices take the place of gravy, which makes it all the more relaxing as it is one less task.

Serves 4

extra virgin olive oil
2 tablespoons lemon juice
½ teaspoon paprika
¼ teaspoon allspice
1 tablespoon thyme leaves
1 x 1.6kg free-range chicken,
    untrussed
sea salt

Ideally marinate the chicken overnight, but it isn't the end of the world if you don't. Combine 2 tablespoons of olive oil with the lemon juice, the spices and thyme in a bowl. Spoon this over the chicken in a roasting tin, coating the surface of the skin. If marinating the chicken overnight, cover the dish with clingfilm and chill.

Preheat the oven to 190°C fan/210°C electric/gas 7. Baste the chicken with any juices that have run down into the dish, season with salt and roast for 55 minutes, basting it a couple of times during roasting. Leave the chicken to rest in the tin for 20 minutes.

Remove the chicken to a plate, tipping any juices inside the bird back into the tin, then skim off the excess fat. Carve the chicken and serve with the juices spooned over, accompanied by the salad if wished.
Carbohydrate 0.7g Protein 50.6g

WITH FATTOUSH
This salad usually contains bread, but it is just as delightful without – the vegetables as an ensemble are crisp and clean, and you can add diced feta and olives to pan it out too. This makes a large bowlful, which I find is not overdoing it for three or four, even though at a glance it easily serves six.

Serves 4

1 cucumber, peeled, halved
    lengthways and thickly sliced
200g radishes, trimmed and
    quartered
300g baby plum or cherry
    tomatoes, halved
1 small red onion, peeled, halved
    and thinly sliced
a large handful each of mint leaves
    and flat-leaf parsley
3 tablespoons extra virgin olive oil
2 tablespoons lemon juice
sea salt

Place the cucumber, radishes and tomatoes in a large bowl with the onion, separating out the strands. Tear the mint leaves in half and coarsely chop the parsley, and toss with the salad vegetables. You can prepare the salad to this point in advance, in which case cover the vegetables with clingfilm and set aside somewhere cool.

Just before eating, pour the oil and lemon juice over the vegetables, season with salt and toss.
Carbohydrate 4.7g Protein 51.9g

Roast chicken with a watercress crust

Don't be alarmed by the amount of butter given over to roasting, it mainly serves to baste the bird as it cooks and is spooned off at the end. The watercress makes for a thick, succulent bank of stuffing beneath the skin, and is far more delicate than a breadcrumb stuffing inside the bird.

Serves 6

1 lemon
75g unsalted butter, softened
sea salt, black pepper
100g watercress
2 tablespoons capers, rinsed and
    finely chopped
1 x 2kg free-range chicken,
    untrussed

Preheat the oven to 200°C fan/220°C electric/gas 7. Zest the lemon and blend with 50g of the butter and some seasoning in a large bowl. (If your butter is on the hard side, cream it in a food processor first.) Give the watercress a quick whizz in a clean food processor to finely chop it, and work into the butter with the capers. Using your hands, gently squeeze out the excess liquid.

Starting at the neck end of the chicken slip your fingers beneath the skin to loosen it over the breasts. Gently smooth half the watercress butter over each breast and pat the skin back into place, spreading the butter out evenly. Rub the remaining butter over the chicken. Place it in a roasting tin that accommodates it quite snugly, halve the lemon and squeeze the juice over the bird, pop the halves inside the cavity, then season.

Roast for 1 hour then remove the chicken from the oven and transfer to a warm plate to rest for 15–20 minutes, tipping any juices inside the bird back into the tin. Skim any fat off the roasting juices, add about 6 tablespoons of water and simmer, taking up all the sticky residue from the base, then pass through a sieve. Carve the chicken, adding any juices that have collected to the gravy.
Carbohydrate 0.4g Protein 42.7g

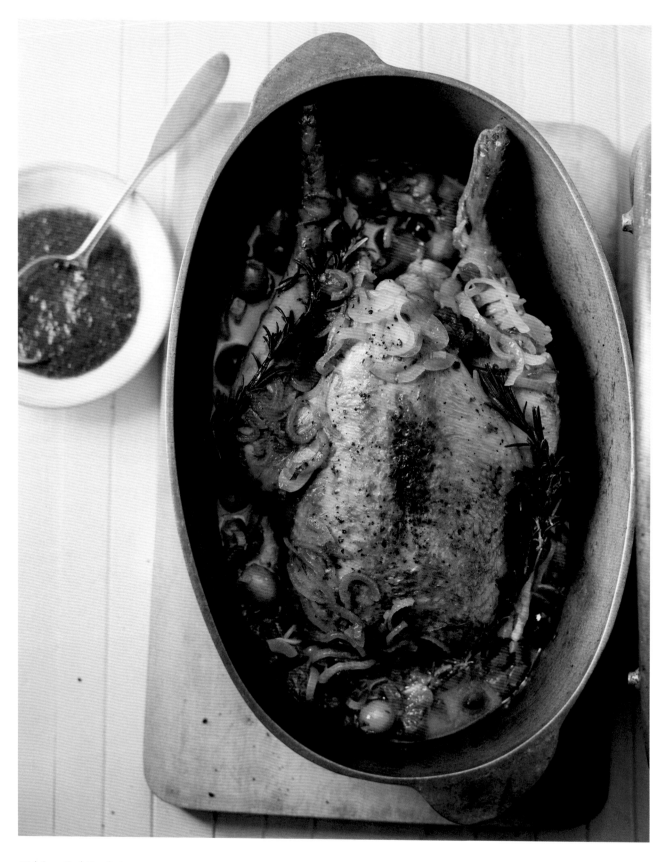

Provençal pot-roast with pistou

Pot-roasts are brilliant at providing the gravy or a sauce, as well as making for a particularly succulent bird as it is 'wet-roasted'. This one, with its Mediterranean flair of tomatoes, olives and basil, has the edge over pot-roasts that come laced with crème fraîche and thickened with flour.

Serves 4

2 beefsteak tomatoes
extra virgin olive oil
1 x 1.6kg free-range chicken, untrussed
sea salt, black pepper
3 medium or 2 large onions, peeled, halved and sliced
3 garlic cloves, peeled and finely sliced
2 sprigs of fresh rosemary
1 small dried red chilli, finely chopped
150ml white wine
4 large handfuls of basil leaves
150g pitted green and black olives

Bring a medium saucepan of water to the boil. Cut out a cone from the centre of each tomato, plunge them into the water for about 20 seconds and then into cold water. Slip off the skins and coarsely chop them.

Heat a large cast-iron casserole over a medium–high heat. Pour a little olive oil into the palm of your hand, rub your hands together and coat the chicken all over. Season it with salt and pepper and place in the casserole to colour on all sides. Remove it to a plate and turn the heat down. Add another couple of tablespoons of oil and fry the onions for about 5 minutes, stirring frequently, until softened and translucent – they may colour a little. Once the heat calms down you can turn it up a little. Add the garlic a minute or so before the end.

Add the tomatoes, the rosemary, chilli, wine and some salt, and settle the chicken into the sauce. Bring the liquid to a simmer, cover and cook over a low heat for 1 hour. While the chicken is cooking, place the basil leaves in a food processor with 9 tablespoons of olive oil and a little salt and reduce to a purée.

Remove the chicken from the oven and transfer to a warm plate, tipping any juices inside the bird back into the tin, and leave to rest for 15 minutes. Leave the sauce to stand for 5–10 minutes for the oil to rise, then skim it off and reduce the juices by half to concentrate the flavour. Carve the chicken and serve with the sauce spooned over, and a little of the pistou, scattered with olives.
Carbohydrate 14.9g Protein 52.5g

Rare roast beef with gravy

Thin slices of rare beef and a river of golden gravy is a kitchen essential. This less traditional method of roasting a joint is my default, the lower temperature makes for supremely tender meat and elevates lesser roasting joints, making it great for silverside as well as the sirloin suggested here, which is for more of a special treat.

Serves 6

Beef:
1 tablespoon groundnut or
   vegetable oil
1.5kg joint of sirloin
1 scant teaspoon English mustard
   powder
sea salt, black pepper
1 heaped tablespoon grainy
   mustard

Preheat the oven to 130°C fan/150°C electric/gas 2. Heat the oil in a large frying pan with a heatproof handle over a high heat. Use a tea strainer to dust the fat and underside of the joint with the mustard powder, and season it. Sear on all four sides until golden – the ends too – it should be well-coloured as you're roasting at a low temperature. Brush half the grainy mustard over the bottom of the joint with a pastry brush, and the rest over the top. Transfer the beef in the frying pan to the oven and roast for 50 minutes to leave it rare, then remove from the oven, loosely cover with foil and leave it to rest for 20 minutes. (I have a habit of forgetting that the handle of the pan is hot, so leaving a tea towel wrapped around it isn't a bad idea.) Thinly carve and serve with the gravy. The cold meat is also great sandwich material.
Carbohydrate 0.4g Protein 51.2g

GRAVY

For an even richer flavour, you could use a little Madeira or medium sherry in lieu of the same amount of red wine here.

Gravy:
2 tablespoons groundnut or
   vegetable oil
500g mixture of diced onion,
   celery, carrot and leek
2 garlic cloves, peeled and finely
   chopped
150ml red wine
400ml beef stock

Heat the oil in a large saucepan over a medium heat, add the vegetables and fry for 30–35 minutes, stirring occasionally, until really well coloured, almost black (this is your gravy browning). Add the garlic a few minutes before the end, and then gradually pour in the red wine, and cook for a couple of minutes. Stir in the stock in two or three goes, add some seasoning and simmer for about 5 minutes. Pass the gravy through a sieve, pressing out as much as possible from the vegetables. If it tastes at all thin, you can simmer it a few minutes longer, and check the seasoning. If you let it stand for any length of time, then there may be a little oil on the surface, which you can skim off. Add any juices given out when you slice the beef.
Carbohydrate 5.2g Protein 52.3g

THICKENED GRAVY
If you want to thicken the gravy slightly, add 2 teaspoons of **flour** to the pan after frying the veg, then add the wine and cook, stirring, for a couple of minutes until it thickens.
Carbohydrate 6.5g Protein 52.5g

Roast beef with beetroot and horseradish sauce

Here the beef roasts in a relatively high oven, which is traditional, with lots of syrupy sweet onions and beetroot, the secret being to slice the beetroot thinly enough. The vegetables are quite good-natured and won't come to any harm if you need to cook the beef a little more or less, depending on the size of the joint and how you like it cooked.

Serves 4

700g beetroot, peeled and cut into thin wedges
4 tablespoons extra virgin olive oil
sea salt, black pepper
4 red onions, peeled, halved and thinly sliced
800g joint of silverside
1 tablespoon balsamic vinegar
6 tablespoons coarsely chopped flat-leaf parsley

Preheat the oven to 180°C fan/200°C electric/gas 6. For an 800g joint, allow 30–40 minutes for the beef to leave it medium-rare to medium, so the beetroot will take 60–70 minutes in total. Arrange the beetroot in a large roasting tin (about 25 x 38cm), pour over 2 tablespoons of olive oil, season and toss, and cook for 20 minutes.

Scatter the onions over the beetroot, drizzle over another couple of tablespoons of oil, season and give the vegetables a stir, then roast for another 10 minutes. At the same time, heat a large frying pan over a high heat, season the beef and sear to colour all over, starting with the fat side.

Drizzle the balsamic vinegar over the vegetables and give them a stir, nestle the beef fat-side up in the centre and roast for another 30–40 minutes or until a meat thermometer reads 50–52°C for medium-rare, and 55–60°C for medium after several minutes. Remove from the oven, loosely cover the tin with foil and leave to rest for 15 minutes. Thinly carve the beef. Stir the parsley into the vegetables, and serve with the beef and the horseradish cream.
Carbohydrate 24.2g Protein 45.5g

WITH HORSERADISH CREAM
Blend 100g **low-fat crème fraîche** with 1–2 teaspoons of **horseradish sauce** in a bowl and season with **sea salt**.
Carbohydrate 25.5g Protein 46.2g

Duck à l'orange

An oldie but a goodie, updated. It's easy to see why this fruit is so often paired with duck, slicing through that louche richness. If the season allows, this is even better made with blood oranges.

Serves 4

Duck:
1 x 2kg oven-ready duck,
    untrussed, ideally with giblets
sea salt, black pepper
150ml orange juice
250ml giblet or chicken stock
watercress to serve

Roast onions:
4 red onions, peeled and cut into
    slim wedges
2 whole oranges, sliced, ends
    discarded
1 cinnamon stick
2 star anise
2 bay leaves
about 3 tablespoons rendered
    duck fat
duck liver (if included), fatty
    membranes removed and diced

Preheat the oven to 210°C fan/230°C electric/gas 8. Pat the duck dry using kitchen paper, prick all over using the tip of a sharp knife and season a little more generously than usual with salt, rubbing it into the skin. Place it breast-side down on a roasting rack in a large roasting tray and roast for 1¾ hours. Drain off the fat after 1 hour (this can be used for roasting the onions), but without basting – you may find it easiest to transfer the duck and rack to a plate first – then turn the bird breast-side up.

At the end of roasting, place the duck on the rack over a large plate, tipping any juices inside the bird back into the tin, and leave to rest for 15 minutes. Drain the excess fat off the roasting tray, add the orange juice and simmer to reduce by about half, scraping up all the sticky residue from the base of the tin. Add the stock and continue to simmer until nicely rich, then taste for seasoning. Carve and serve the duck with the gravy, watercress and onions.
Carbohydrate 3.9g Protein 27.7g

Arrange the onions and orange slices in a large roasting pan with the spices and bay leaves. After an hour of cooking the duck, at the same time you drain off the fat, drizzle 3 tablespoons over the onions and roast for 55–60 minutes (to include the resting time for the bird), stirring halfway through. If you happen to have the duck liver, then heat a teaspoon of the duck fat in a small frying pan over a medium–high heat. Add the liver, season and fry for about 1 minute to seal it on the outside, while leaving it rare within, tossing constantly. Serve this scattered over the onions, discarding the orange and aromatics.
Carbohydrate 19.9g Protein 31.4g

Slow-roast salt and pepper duck

Like Peking duck, this has everything to do with the delicate sheaves of crisp skin, so sprightly sautéed greens seem just the ticket alongside, but these aren't a must. It's a great way of cooking duck whatever you want to accompany it with. Two heads of spring cabbage may provide a little more than you want, so bear in mind frying it up afterwards with some root veg in all that lovely duck fat given out during the slow roasting.

Serves 4

Duck:
1 x 2.2–2.5kg oven-ready duck, untrussed, ideally with giblets
sea salt, black pepper
a handful each of fresh sage leaves and thyme sprigs
100ml medium sherry
400ml giblet or chicken stock

Spring greens:
2 heads of spring greens
extra virgin olive oil
freshly grated nutmeg

Preheat the oven to 140°C fan/160°C electric/gas 3. Generously season the duck all over, rubbing the salt and pepper into the skin, and stuff the cavity with the herbs. Place the duck breast-side up (ideally on a rack) in a roasting tin and roast for 3 hours, draining the fat into a bowl at roughly hourly intervals for the first couple of hours.

While the duck is roasting slice the greens across as finely as possible, discarding the tough stalks at the base. Give them a wash in a sink of cold water, and then a whirl in a salad spinner to dry them off.

Turn up the oven temperature to 200°C fan/220°C electric/gas 7 and roast the duck for a further 15 minutes to colour and crisp the skin. Remove from the oven and transfer the duck on the rack to a warm plate, tipping any juices back into the tin, and leave to rest for 15 minutes while you make the gravy and cook the greens.

Skim any excess fat off the roasting tin, add the sherry and simmer for several minutes until it is well reduced, scraping up any sticky residue from the bottom. Add the stock, bring to the boil and simmer for several minutes until rich and amalgamated, then season to taste and pour into a warm jug or gravy boat.

At the same time fry the greens in batches. Heat either a tablespoon of the rendered duck fat or olive oil in a large frying pan over a high heat, add a pile of the greens, season with salt and nutmeg and sauté until they wilt and start to colour, then remove them to a warm serving bowl and cook the remainder in the same way.

Carve the duck, or loosely pull it apart, making sure you get all of the skin – it should be crisp both top and bottom. Serve with the spring greens and gravy.
Carbohydrate 5.5g Protein 33.3g

THICKENED GRAVY
Stir in 1 tablespoon of **flour** after adding the sherry and allow it to seethe momentarily, then gradually blend in the stock, and pass through a sieve into the jug or gravy boat.
Carbohydrate 8.6g Protein 33.7g

Chilli roast pork belly

All those lovely succulent strips of meat, the caramelised edges and crispy crackling…. This can be as indulgent or restrained as you choose, that is, you don't 'have to' eat the fat or the crackling.

Serves 4

Marinade:
1 medium-hot red chilli, core and
    seeds discarded
7cm fresh ginger, peeled and cut up
4 garlic cloves, peeled
1 heaped teaspoon ground
    coriander
1 heaped teaspoon ground cumin
$1/3$ teaspoon cayenne pepper
1 tablespoon vegetable oil

Pork:
1 x 1.8kg pork belly joint,
    preferably ribs-in, skin cut
    off and scored at 1cm intervals
sea salt

1 tablespoon vegetable oil
500–600g choi sum, base trimmed,
    cut into lengths a few cm long
200ml chicken stock

Put all the marinade ingredients in a food processor and whizz to a paste. Rub this into the pork joint on either side, at the ends, and into any crevices. Place the joint, ribs down, in a large roasting tin, cover and chill for 1 hour.

Preheat the oven to 200°C fan/220°C electric/gas 7. Season the joint on both sides with salt and pour a glass of water into the base of the pan. Place the skin rind-up in another roasting tin, again seasoning with salt. Roast the joint for 2 hours with the crackling below, turning down the oven temperature to 150°C fan/170°C electric/gas 3 after 30 minutes. Remove the joint from the oven and transfer to a warm plate to rest for 20 minutes, and turn the oven back up to 200°C fan/220°C electric/gas 7 to crisp the crackling for another 15–20 minutes.

Carve the belly between the ribs, halving the strips if long, and serve with the choi sum and gravy, and the crackling.
Carbohydrate 2.1g Protein 72.2g

WITH CHOI SUM
Place the roasting tin used for the belly over a medium heat, add the oil and fry the choi sum stalks for a couple of minutes until glossy and starting to relax, then stir in the leaves, add the stock and simmer for a couple of minutes, incorporating all the caramelised bits from the base of the pan.
Carbohydrate 4.9g Protein 75.6g

SIMPLY ROAST PORK
For an easy Sunday or week-day roast a rolled pork shoulder makes for fine eating. I like to rub it with spices, which makes for particularly alluring and tasty golden edges. There is no call for gravy here, just some roast veg, perhaps a mash or green salad.

Ask your butcher for the skin to be removed, and the **pork shoulder** to be rolled and tied. Rub the meat with a **spice blend** such as za'atar, a masala or La Kama (another one from Seasoned Pioneers – see page 14) and season with **sea salt** and **black pepper**. Place the skin, rind-side up, in a separate roasting tin and rub with salt. Roast the two for 15 minutes at 230°C fan/250°C electric/gas 8, then reduce the temperature to 160°C fan/180°C electric/gas 4, and continue to roast for 55–65 minutes per kg or until the meat registers 72–75°C on a meat thermometer. Leave the crackling in the oven while the meat rests for 20 minutes. A 1.5 kg joint (weighed with the rind) will serve 4–6.
Carbohydrate 1.4g Protein 67.2g

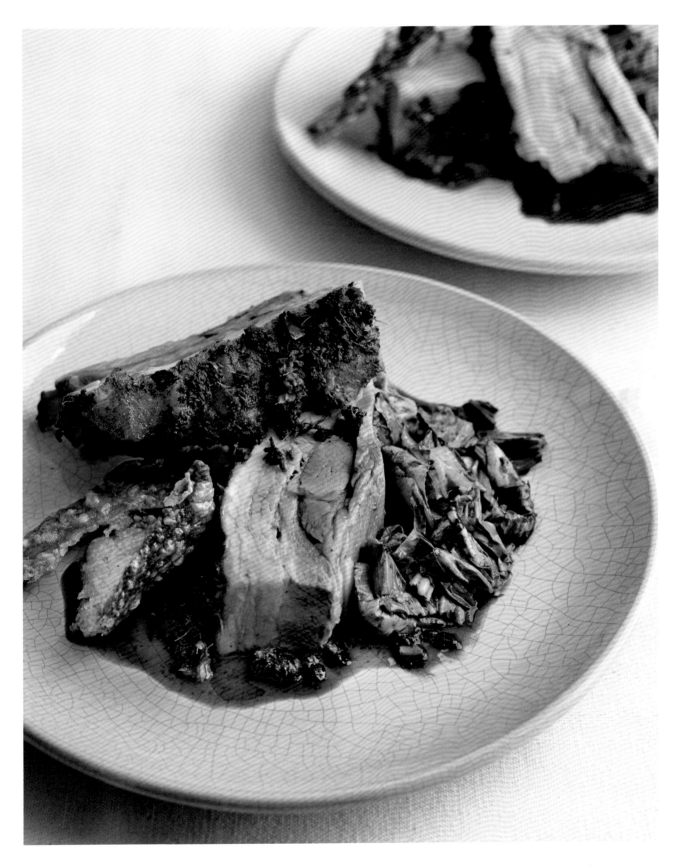

Leg of lamb roasted with anchovies

The notion of anchovies with lamb seems wholly unlikely, and yet there is no hint of these salty little fish by the time the meat is roasted, they simply add another dimension or depth to the flavour. A leg of lamb doesn't have to mean feeding a large number of people, a small one weighing about 1.6–1.7kg is perfect for four. At least, that is your week-day excuse.

Serves 4

Lamb:
1 leg of lamb (about 1.7kg), knuckle removed
4–5 salted anchovies, cut into 1cm nibs
a handful of fresh thyme sprigs
extra virgin olive oil
sea salt, black pepper

Courgettes:
4 small courgettes (about 600g), ends discarded, thickly sliced diagonally
1 tablespoon lemon juice
1 garlic clove, peeled and crushed to a paste
a handful of mint leaves, torn

Preheat the oven to 230°C fan/250°C electric/gas 9. Make small slits all over the lamb flesh using a sharp knife, then with the help of the tip of a teaspoon handle insert a nib of anchovy into each one. Put the thyme sprigs in a roasting tin that will accommodate the lamb snugly. Drizzle some olive oil all over the lamb, season the joint and place, fat-side up, on top of the thyme in the tin. You can also tuck the knuckle bone under the edge of the joint. Roast for 15 minutes, then turn down the oven temperature to 160°C fan/180°C electric/gas 4 and cook for a further 33 minutes per kg for medium. Remove from the oven and leave the lamb to rest in a warm place for 15–20 minutes. Carve the lamb across the grain and serve with the courgettes.

While the lamb is cooking, heat a couple of tablespoons of oil in a large frying pan over a medium–high heat, add the courgettes, season and fry until coloured on either side but remaining slightly crisp. Whisk the lemon juice with the garlic and some seasoning in a small bowl, then whisk in 3 tablespoons of oil. Pour this over the courgettes in a bowl, leave to cool for about 10 minutes, then mix in the mint. This can be served warm or at room temperature.
Carbohydrate 3.5g Protein 65.8g

Butterflied leg of lamb

The first time I ordered this cut in my local butcher in Normandy, the French term for 'butterflied' escaped me, and I found myself directing the filleting cut by cut, like a surgeon overseeing an emergency operation. It is basically a leg that has been boned and opened out, and it cooks up like a big juicy fillet. Not only does it lend itself to being marinated but also barbecued. Weber kettles are brilliant for cooking large cuts – whole chickens, fish and legs of lamb, here I would allow 50–60 minutes for a 2kg butterflied leg.

Serves 6

Marinade:
2 bay leaves, torn into pieces
1 teaspoon fresh thyme leaves
3 shallots, peeled and finely
    chopped
3 garlic cloves, peeled and crushed
    to a paste
3 tablespoons vegetable oil
3 tablespoons Calvados or brandy

Lamb:
1 butterflied leg of lamb
    (about 2.5kg)
sea salt, black pepper

Combine all the marinade ingredients in a large bowl or roasting tin. Open out the butterflied leg of lamb, place it in the bowl or tin and using your hands coat both sides with the marinade. Cover it with clingfilm and chill for several hours, or overnight.

Bring the leg back up to room temperature for 1 hour before cooking. Preheat the oven to 200°C fan/220°C electric/gas 7. Season the marinated joint on both sides and place it, fat-side up, in a large roasting dish, opening it out. Roast for 20 minutes per kg – less than you would normally cook a leg for, to allow for the fact that it has been boned and opened out.

Baste the meat halfway through.

Remove the lamb from the oven and leave it to rest in a warm place for 20 minutes, then transfer it to a carving plate. Skim the excess fat from the roasting tin – there should be plenty of juices – and heat to a simmer, scraping up all the sticky residue from the base of the tin, then add a drop of water to achieve a tasty jus. Carve the lamb across the grain, adding any juices given out as it rested to the gravy.

Carbohydrate 0.7g Protein 81.1g

Kleftiko

The romantic outward-bound origins of this dish lie with Greek bandits, who would slow-roast their stolen meat or *kleftiko* in a sealed hole in the ground, to conceal the sweet aromas of dinner cooking from their pursuers. And whatever happened in between, today it refers to lamb or goat cooked in a sealed parcel, and we love it for that reason alone. The lamb meat infuses with oregano and garlic as it roasts. Feta at the end is optional, but it does go particularly well with the lemon and herbs.

Serves 6

1 shoulder of lamb (about 2–2.2kg)
extra virgin olive oil
sea salt, black pepper
a small bunch of fresh oregano, (about 20g)
¼ teaspoon ground cinnamon
2 heads of garlic, tops cut off and individual cloves separated
juice of 1 lemon
200g feta, diced (optional)

Preheat the oven to 120°C fan/140°C electric/gas 1. Heat a large frying pan over a medium–high heat. Using your hands lightly coat the lamb with oil, season and sear to colour it all over.

Now make a parcel by laying two long sheets of baking paper one on top of the other at right angles. You want to allow enough spare at the ends to be able to pleat the edges together 2–3 times and leave a pocket of air within, once the lamb is inside. Pull off some of the oregano leaves and scatter half the leaves and sprigs in the centre of the paper. Drizzle over a little oil and place the lamb on top. Dust with cinnamon, scatter over the remaining oregano leaves and sprigs, then scatter the garlic cloves over and around the joint. Drizzle with more oil and the lemon juice and then seal the parcel by bringing the opposite sides to the centre and pleating together. Place the parcel in a roasting tin and roast for 5 hours until the meat is meltingly tender.

If you are serving it with the feta, turn up the oven temperature to 200°C fan/220°C electric/gas 7, open the paper at the top, scatter over the cheese, baste everything with the juices and return to the oven for 10 minutes. Skim off any excess fat from the juices before serving.
Carbohydrate 1.9g Protein 53.4g

FRESH FISH DAILY

12·90

THE FISH SHOP

The Chippie, now there's a challenge. Fish fried in batter, fishcakes with more potato than fish, AND coated in breadcrumbs, a pie with butter, cream, tiny bit of fish and lots of mash, and chips, chips and more chips. Personally, because I've never eaten fried food, I find the idea of it offputting. I remember my son telling my mum, when he was about twelve, that he had never had fish and chips. You would have thought from her reaction that I had committed some terrible crime: 'Poor child, you poor, poor child.' And she swore to right it at our very next visit, which she did, and then proceeded to order in fish and chips almost every time we went to see her. It wasn't that I hadn't ever given him fish and chips on principle, I just don't particularly like them, so it had never occurred to me.

And I do think that if you change your eating habits for a healthier regime, that eventually you go off the foods you have left behind. A sweet tooth recedes once you give up sugar in your tea, and if you are unaccustomed to eating shop-bought milk chocolate and biscuits, they are unpalatably overwhelming.

So part of the journey is about accepting this shift. These dishes may not convince the diehard who will only settle for the original dish, but approach them with an open mind and accept them as being delicious in their own right, and there is plenty of fine feasting to be done.

The ultimate prawn cocktail

However hackneyed – and over the years it has been abused more than most dishes – Prawn Cocktail never dates. Well made, it is a gorgeous big splash of an affair, where very finely sliced chilled lettuce is layered with prawns and a homemade cocktail sauce. Restaurants like the Wolseley in Piccadilly keep the flame alive with their ice-cold silvered cocktail dishes filled to the brim (they do crab and lobster too – just as good), and this recipe is very much based on their tradition.

Serves 4

Sauce Marie Rose:
1 medium organic egg yolk
1 scant teaspoon Dijon mustard
75ml groundnut oil
1 tablespoon tomato ketchup
a shake or two of Tabasco sauce

Vinaigrette:
1 teaspoon Dijon mustard
sea salt, black pepper
3 tablespoons groundnut oil
1 teaspoon lemon juice

Prawns:
400g coldwater prawns, cooked
    and peeled
a generous squeeze of lemon juice
2 tablespoons finely chopped
    flat-leaf parsley, plus a little
    extra to serve
1 Iceberg lettuce, chilled, base
    trimmed
3 slim spring onions, trimmed and
    finely sliced

To prepare the sauce, whisk the egg yolk with the mustard in a medium bowl, then gradually whisk in the oil, a few drops at a time to begin with, until the mayonnaise takes. Stir in the tomato ketchup, then season with Tabasco; I like a noticeable nip of chilli.

To make the vinaigrette, whisk the mustard with a little seasoning in a medium bowl, then whisk in the oil a tablespoon at a time, until it is thick and mayonnaise-like. Stir in the lemon juice and then 2–4 teaspoons of water to thin the vinaigrette to the consistency of single cream.

Toss the prawns in a bowl with a generous squeeze of lemon, a little black pepper and the parsley. Quarter the lettuce downwards, then halve each quarter across and slice as finely as possible into grass-like strands using a sharp knife. Combine this in another bowl with the spring onions, and toss with the vinaigrette.

Divide half the lettuce between four deep cupped bowls or sundae glasses, scatter over half the prawns, drizzle a teaspoon of the Marie Rose sauce over each one, and repeat the layers, then scatter over a little more parsley.
Carbohydrate 3.4g Protein 24.4g

SPEEDY COCKTAIL SAUCE
You can also make a speedy low-fat cocktail sauce with 100g **low-fat fromage frais**, 1 tablespoon **mayonnaise**, 1 tablespoon **tomato ketchup** and a little **sea salt**.
Carbohydrate 5.4g Protein 25g

Salade Niçoise

There is something about a *Salade Niçoise* that gives you the same kind of feeling of being as satiated as if had you eaten a steak. Perhaps not suprisingly, as the combination of tuna, eggs and olives is a cocktail of superfoods. On a hungry day, a can of tuna, which can be dressed up with a squeeze of lemon, some chopped parsley and finely sliced chilli, is a blessing of a high-protein snack.

Given the number of storecupboard ingredients this calls for, it makes a regular appearance in our house, not least because fresh tuna is off the menu on sustainable grounds, so jars of sustainable Albacore that promise big meaty flakes of pinkish ivory fish are a great luxury fall-back. Rarefied Spanish delis also make a good hunting ground for tuna that is a cut above the norm.

Serves 4

4 medium eggs
6 tablespoons extra virgin olive oil
1½ tablespoons lemon juice
sea salt, black pepper
2 tablespoons small capers
   (eg nonpareille), rinsed
2 x 200g jars or cans of tuna in
   springwater, drained
4 salted anchovy fillets, halved
   lengthways
3 ripe plum or speciality tomatoes,
   cores removed, cut into wedges
70g pitted green or black olives
70–80g rocket leaves

Bring a medium pan of water to the boil, add the eggs and boil for 7–8 minutes to leave them slightly wet in the centre, then drain and cool in cold water.

Whisk the olive oil, lemon juice, some seasoning and the capers in a large deep salad bowl, one that gives you enough room for tossing once you have layered all the ingredients. Dry the tuna on a double thickness of kitchen paper, then break it into chunks or coarse flakes. Add to the dressing, and turn to coat everything. Lay the anchovy fillets on top, then the tomatoes and scatter over the olives. Finally pile the rocket on top. Cover with clingfilm and set aside in a cool place.

To serve, shell and quarter the eggs. Gently turn the salad over a couple of times, and arrange the eggs on top.
Carbohydrate 2.9g Protein 25g

Whole mackerel roasted with cherry tomatoes and olives

We are inclined to give this fish the northerly treatment by marrying it off with sharp fruit sauces like gooseberry and rhubarb, or coat it in oatmeal, but it is equally at home with sunnier fare like tomatoes on the vine, olives, rocket and balsamic vinegar. It does, after all, have something akin to sardines about it, in fact pretty much any way that you might cook these will also translate to mackerel.

Serves 4

4 x whole mackerel (about 300g each), cleaned
extra virgin olive oil
sea salt, black pepper
500g cherry tomatoes on the vine
1 tablespoon balsamic vinegar
100g pitted black olives
4 large handfuls of rocket

Preheat the oven to 220°C fan/240°C electric/gas 9. Score the mackerel flesh diagonally at 3–4cm intervals on both sides, brush with oil and season. Heat a large, non-stick frying pan over a medium–high heat and sear the mackerel, one at a time, for 1 minute on each side, then arrange them head to tail in a roasting dish. Lay the tomatoes on top, drizzle over 2 tablespoons of oil, and the balsamic vinegar and roast for 15 minutes. Scatter over the olives and leave to stand for 5 minutes. Serve with any juices spooned over. Pile some rocket on top or to the side of each mackerel and drizzle over a little more oil. *Carbohydrate 5.4g Protein 44.4g*

SIMPLY MACKEREL FILLETS
Mackerel fillets are a great suppertime basic, loaded with goodness and all those fish oils, and they only take some 5 minutes to cook. One of my favourite ways of eating these is to dress some cooked and diced beetroot with olive oil and balsamic vinegar, throw in a little chopped dill and pile this on top of watercress.

Heat a teaspoon of **extra virgin olive oil** in a large, non-stick frying pan over a medium heat. Season 600–800g **mackerel fillets** (ideally 4) on either side, and fry half at a time skin-side down for about 3 minutes until golden and crispy, and the flesh is cooked through by about two-thirds, then turn and cook for 1 minute longer on the flesh-side. Remove these to a plate and cook the rest in the same way. *Carbohydrate 0g Protein 28.1g*

Moules marinière

Moules Marinière is at heart an elementary dish, and it's a sign of the times that we tend to trick it up, more rare to encounter the original than some fusion take on it. But the original is by far and away still the best, especially if you happen to be eating it in the environs of mussel beds, something my family is spoiled with at our house in Normandy, because an extensive marine park fringes our coastline.

At the beachside restaurant La Cale, in Blainville-sur-Mer, from where this recipe derives, there will be about five pots on the go at any one time, with the waiting table's number written in felt pen on the lid. The chips they serve with them are about the only sort that I am ever tempted to eat – and do – skinny and crisp with hundreds of deliciously crunchy splinters of potato. But here we will do without.

Serves 2

1.7kg fresh mussels
3 tablespoons groundnut or
    vegetable oil
2 tablespoons very finely chopped
    onion
2 tablespoons very finely chopped
    shallot
1 garlic clove, peeled and finely
    chopped
100ml white wine
70g low-fat crème fraîche
a handful coarsely chopped flat-leaf
    parsley

Give the mussels a good wash in a sink of cold water, discarding any that are broken or that do not close when tapped. Pull off any beards and scrape off any barnacles. If very dirty, give them a second rinse.

Heat the oil in a large saucepan over a high heat, add the onion, shallot and garlic and fry for about 1 minute until softened, then pour in the wine and simmer to reduce by half. Add the mussels, clamp on the lid and cook for 5–6 minutes until opened. Stir in the crème fraîche and parsley and serve at once.
Carbohydrate 13.5g Protein 33.6g

Salmon, prawn and tomato stew

This delicous stew was designed with accessibility in mind, given that so often fish stews require hunting around for the right species, but the caveat is that they are responsibly farmed. You can also use queen scallops here in lieu of salmon, their gristle removed, in which case halve the quantity and the poaching time.

Serves 4

500g plum tomatoes
extra virgin olive oil
5 shallots, peeled, halved and sliced
1 celery heart, trimmed and sliced
2 teaspoons finely chopped
    medium-hot red chilli
sea salt, black pepper
a large pinch of saffron filaments,
    (about 20)
300ml fish stock
450g salmon fillet, skinned and cut
    into 2cm pieces
200g raw peeled prawns
coarsely chopped flat-leaf parsley,
    to serve

Bring a medium pan of water to the boil, cut out a cone from the top of each tomato, dunk them into the boiling water for 20 seconds and then into cold water. Slip off the skins and coarsely chop them.

Heat 2 tablespoons of olive oil in a large saucepan over a medium heat and fry the shallots for several minutes until softened. Add the celery and chilli and fry for a further 5–7 minutes until glossy and relaxed.

Add the tomatoes and some salt and cook for about 8 minutes, pressing the tomatoes down until you have a textured purée. Add the saffron and the fish stock, bring to the boil and simmer over a low heat for 10 minutes. The stew can be prepared to this point in advance.

To serve, bring the stock base back to the boil. Season the salmon and add to the pan, together with the prawns, and poach for 5 minutes. Serve the stew scattered with chopped parsley.
Carbohydrate 5.4g Protein 33.6g

Cod, crayfish, spinach and coriander stew

This has Portuguese aspirations with its dark green spinach leaves, tender lily-white cod and snippets of bacon, and the wild card of lots of fresh coriander. But as with any fish stew, the fish is merely a suggestion: read cod to mean anything white and meaty, the more obscure and less sought after the better.

Serves 6

50g unsalted butter
3 large onions, peeled, quartered
    and thinly sliced across
sea salt, black pepper
150ml white wine
900ml chicken stock
500g spinach leaves, sliced if large
50g coriander leaves and fine stalks,
    coarsely chopped, plus extra to
    serve
1 teaspoon vegetable oil
6 rashers rindless unsmoked back
    bacon, diced
600g cod loin (skinned weight),
    cut into 2–4cm dice
300g cooked and peeled crayfish,
    or king prawns

Melt the butter in a large saucepan over a lowish heat, add the onions, scatter over a teaspoon of salt and fry for 15–20 minutes, stirring occasionally, until soft and syrupy without allowing them to colour more than a little. Add the wine, turn up the heat and cook to reduce it by half. Pour in the chicken stock and bring to the boil, then add the spinach, half the coriander and some seasoning. Bring the stock back to the boil, then cover the pan and cook over a low heat for 10 minutes, stirring the stock after a couple of minutes to submerge the leaves.

Briefly whizz two-thirds of the vegetables in a food processor to break them up, then return these to the pan. The stew can be prepared to this point in advance.

Shortly before serving, heat the oil in a large, non-stick frying pan over a medium heat and fry the bacon for 5–7 minutes until lightly golden, stirring frequently and separating out the pieces, then drain on a double thickness of kitchen paper. Bring the stock base back to the boil, add the cod, cover and simmer for 2 minutes. Add the crayfish or prawns, half the bacon and the remaining coriander and cook for 1 minute longer. Serve the stew scattered with extra coriander and the remaining bacon.

Carbohydrate 11.9g Protein 40.2g

Cod, beetroot and mint bake

Cod and beetroot make a classic northerly marriage, but given a roasting as a traybake invites in a little sunshine, here with caramelised onions, garlic and orange.

Serves 4

finely grated zest of 1 orange
2 garlic cloves, peeled and crushed to a paste
6 tablespoons extra virgin olive oil
600g cod loin (skinned weight), cut into 8 pieces
700–800g beetroot
2 red onions, peeled, halved and sliced across
sea salt, black pepper

Blend the orange zest and garlic with 3 tablespoons of oil in a large bowl, add the cod and stir to coat it, then cover and chill for 1 hour.

Preheat the oven to 220°C fan/240°C electric/gas 9. Without peeling the beetroot, trim the tops and bottoms of shoots and roots, and cut into wedges. Arrange these in a large roasting tin (about 25 x 38cm) with the onions, pour over 3 tablespoons of olive oil and season. Cover with foil and roast for 30 minutes, then uncover, stir the vegetables and roast for a further 25 minutes.

Five minutes before the end of this time, heat a large, non-stick frying pan over a high heat, season and sear the pieces of cod in two batches for 30 seconds on either side to lightly colour them. Stir the vegetables and tuck the fish in between, and return to the oven for 5 minutes.
Carbohydrate 18.8g Protein 31.4g

WITH MINT SAUCE
You may not need all of this sauce, but it makes a lovely dip for *crudités* thereafter.

While the bake is cooking, blend together 200g **sour cream**, 2 heaped tablespoons finely chopped **mint**, 1½ teaspoons **Dijon mustard** and a pinch of **sea salt** in a medium bowl. Serve this dolloped on top of the fish and vegetables, with a little extra mint scattered over.
Carbohydrate 21.2g Protein 33.2g

Roast lemon sole with sage and onions

Lemon sole is a hugely underrated fish, as sweet and delicate as Dover sole but more down-to-earth. Here the fish are roasted whole with sage leaves and onion.

Serves 2

2 x lemon sole (about 400g), cleaned
50g salted butter, melted
sea salt, black pepper
1 red onion, peeled, halved and finely sliced
a large handful of fresh sage leaves
150ml white wine

Preheat the oven to 200°C fan/220°C electric/gas 7. Score the fish flesh diagonally at 3–4cm intervals on both sides, then brush with the melted butter and season. Heat a large, non-stick frying pan over a medium–high heat, and sear the fish, one at a time, first for 1 minute on the upper side, and then a further minute on the lower side, and slide out into a large roasting tin (about 25 x 38cm). Add the rest of the melted butter to the pan, add the onion and sage leaves and fry for a few minutes, stirring frequently, until just starting to colour, then spoon this over the fish, pour the wine into the bottom of the tin and roast for 15 minutes. I would let everyone fillet their own fish, and serve with the juices spooned over.

Carbohydrate 10.6g Protein 50.9g

Grilled squid with lemon and chilli

The secret to grilling squid is to get your griddle really, really, really hot so that it brands the flesh.

Serves 2
Squid:
450g squid, about the length of your hand
rocket or a mixture of salad leaves containing rocket

Sauce and dressing:
1 tablespoon lemon juice, plus an extra squeeze for the salad
½ teaspoon finely grated lemon zest
1 medium-hot red chilli, core and seeds discarded, and finely chopped
sea salt, black pepper
2 tablespoons extra virgin olive oil, plus extra for squid and salad

First, the task of cleaning your squid. Tug the tentacles away from the pouch to separate them. Pull off the wings and with them the transparent porphyry-coloured film covering the pouch, and discard. Remove the hard pen from inside and as much of the insides as you can. Slit the pouch open from top to bottom, open it out and scrape off any residual white matter. Score the flesh in a criss-cross pattern at 1cm intervals using the sharp tip of a knife and set aside. Cut the tentacles off the body just above the eyes. Rinse and pat dry.

Preheat your griddle on a high heat. Make the sauce by whisking together the tablespoon of lemon juice and the zest, chilli and some salt, then add the oil. Put the salad leaves in a bowl and toss with olive oil to coat them, a squeeze of lemon and the smallest sprinkling of salt.

Brush the squid on both sides with the oil, season and cook for 3 minutes in total, turning it halfway through. As you cook the second side the pieces should curl up and be striped with gold on the outside. Serve the squid with the sauce spooned over, accompanied by the salad.

Carbohydrate 3.7g Protein 24.6g

Salad of grilled salmon with pickled vegetables

This is a slightly unusual dish in that it marries grilled salmon with lightly pickled veg. As an all-in-one dish, it has lots going for it – fish with a salad and dressing. It can be made several hours or even a day in advance of eating. You can also pad it out with other salads; tomato would be good.

Serves 6

Pickled vegetables:
2 tablespoons extra virgin olive oil
1 teaspoon salt
150ml dry white wine
1½ tablespoons white wine vinegar
2 slim carrots, trimmed, peeled and thinly sliced
1 leek, trimmed and thinly sliced
130g small (1–2cm) cauliflower florets
2 bay leaves
3 garlic cloves, peeled and smashed
a large pinch of saffron filaments, (about 20)
a pinch of chilli flakes
½ teaspoon caster sugar

Salmon:
6 x 150g salmon fillets, skin on
extra virgin olive oil
sea salt, black pepper

Put all the pickled vegetables ingredients into a medium saucepan with 150ml water, bring to the boil and simmer for about 20 minutes (ensure the vegetables are submerged), until everything is tender.

Meanwhile, heat a large non-stick frying pan over a medium heat. Brush the salmon fillets with olive oil and season on both sides. You will need to cook them in batches. Fry for 4–6 minutes, skin-side down, until golden and you can see from the sides that the fish is cooked at least halfway through. Turn and fry the flesh side for 1–2 minutes, leaving the fish slightly underdone in the centre; it should still give a little if you press it.

Arrange the fillets skin-side up in a shallow dish that holds them fairly snugly, but with a little space in between. Stir 2 tablespoons of oil into the hot marinade and pour it over the fish, which should be covered by about two-thirds. Loosely cover with clingfilm or foil and leave to cool completely for about 3 hours. The dish can be made up to a day in advance, in which case chill the cooled fish and vegetables and bring back to room temperature an hour before eating.

Carbohydrate 4.8g Protein 31.7g

Crispy salmon and cabbage

Cabbage is potentially a brute of a vegetable, the Eastern bloc in its Communist era together with our own institutions showed us just how, but slice it wafer-fine into a mass of grass-like strands and fry rather than boil it and it is reborn. The bacon brings out the flavour of the salmon, but you could forego this, and yes, you could forego the sauce as well if you're simply after a quickie supper, salmon with cabbage makes for an austere delight.

Serves 6

Salmon:
1 tablespoon extra virgin or
    groundnut oil
finely grated zest of 1 lemon
6 x 150g salmon fillets, skin on

Cabbage:
50g unsalted butter
150g unsmoked rindless streaky
    bacon, diced
1 small white cabbage, outer leaves
    discarded, quartered, core
    removed and finely sliced
1 small Savoy cabbage, outer leaves
    discarded, quartered, core
    removed and finely sliced
sea salt, black pepper

Preheat the oven to 180°C fan/200°C electric/gas 6. Combine the oil and lemon zest in a small bowl, and rub all over the salmon fillets on a plate then set aside for 15 minutes.

Heat half the butter in a large saucepan over a medium-high heat, add the bacon and fry for 5–6 minutes, stirring frequently until it starts to colour, then add half the cabbage and cook for about 4 minutes until wilted but still crisp, seasoning it with black pepper halfway through. Transfer this to a bowl and cook the remaining cabbage in the same way. Add all the cabbage back to the pan.

At the same time as cooking the cabbage, heat a large, non-stick frying pan over a medium-high heat, and season the salmon fillets on both sides. You will probably need to cook them in two batches, first colour the skin for 4–5 minutes, then turn and sear the flesh for 30 seconds, then transfer them to a roasting dish skin-side up, spaced a little way apart. Roast for 6–8 minutes – you can slip a knife through the centre of the thickest fillet to see if it is done; it should be faintly translucent, just cooked.

Reheat the cabbage if necessary, and serve as a bed for the salmon.
Carbohydrate 7.5g Protein 37.4g

WITH MUSTARD CREAM
A luxurious touch for the salmon and cabbage, any left over is delicious with roast beef.

Blend together 150g **sour cream**, 1½ teaspoons **grainy mustard** and 2 teaspoons finely chopped **tarragon** together in a bowl. Cover and chill until required. Serve spooned over the salmon and cabbage.
Carbohydrate 8.5g Protein 38.2g

Shopping with care

As addictions go, there could be worse – and I eat salmon seasoned with Maldon sea salt and black pepper then fried until crisp in its own oil, several days of the week.

In fact, sometimes for breakfast. I always felt slightly embarrassed about eating it so early when all around me were on toast and porridge, until I encountered a Japanese breakfast menu in a London hotel where Salmon Teriyaki came with pickled plums, and I have been indulging at that time of day ever since. It is an addiction that has been with me all of my life – my husband and I always reckon that the reason we knew I was pregnant with our first child was because on a visit to the beautiful Tuscan hill town of Montepulciano, instead of choosing a restaurant for its local specialities I made him traipse around the town looking at menus until he could find one with salmon, such was my craving.

Wild Atlantic salmon was already endangered by the time my habit took hold, so I don't see farmed salmon as being second best; I actively like its softer texture and buttery oiliness. It's delicate and nourishing and leaves you satiated in a particular way. But, there are environmental concerns over intensive salmon farming, and to eat responsibly, we need either to buy organic farmed salmon or that from farms approved by the RSPCA's Freedom Foods scheme. I still believe, however, that in the long term, if the ecological issues can be resolved, farming has to hold the key to taking pressure off wild stocks. It is a comparatively new and emergent industry, so at the same time as applying pressure, I don't think we should be giving up on it. Simply be prepared to pay more for less intensively reared premium brands.

For protein lovers, salmon is one of the most versatile of fish, a great ingredient to have a supply of cooked in the fridge, as good eaten cold as hot, as its texture remains unchanged. It is readily turned into a delicious salad with fine green beans, capers, lemon juice and olive oil, or served with a big green salad with avocado. And it has the edge over smoked salmon, which comes loaded with salt.

Simply fried salmon

I tend to fry my salmon in my largest non-stick saucepan rather than a frying pan, because of the tedium of cleaning up the minute particles of oil that are given off as the fish fries. Alternatively you can cover a frying pan with a lid, leaving a small gap.

Heat a large non-stick frying pan or saucepan over a medium heat, season the top (ie flesh) side of thick, skinned **salmon fillets** weighing about 150g each with **sea salt** and **black pepper**, and fry, top-side down, for about 5 minutes until golden and crispy and you can see the fillets have cooked through by a third to half, then turn and cook the other side for about 3 minutes – exact timings will depend on the thickness of the fillet, but it should have just lost its translucency in the centre.

Carbohydrate 0g Protein 30.3g

Whole roast salmon stuffed with herbs

If you are planning on cooking for a group, roasting up a small whole salmon makes more sense than frying fillets; any left over has nearly as many uses as cold roast chicken, and offers the same ease of cooking. Even though we have salmon year round, quite often there is a glut during the summer, when fish this size abound. You can also make this using sea bass, in which case it may need another 5 minutes cooking.

Serves 4

1 x 1.5kg whole salmon (preferably organic), gutted and scaled, head and tail removed
sea salt, black pepper
4 tablespoons mixture of coarsely chopped fresh dill, flat-leaf parsley and basil
150ml white wine
75g unsalted butter
1 tablespoon small capers, rinsed

Preheat the oven to 200°C fan/220°C electric/gas 7 and preheat the grill. Score the salmon flesh diagonally on both sides at 5cm intervals and season it with salt and pepper, as well as inside the gut cavity. Stuff herbs into the slashes, sprinkling any left over inside the cavity. Line a baking dish or tray that is as long as the salmon with a double layer of foil and lay the fish on top. Grill the salmon for 3–6 minutes on each side until the skin blisters and colours.

Cup the edges of the foil. Pour the wine over the salmon, dot with the butter and roast for 25–30 minutes. Check whether it is cooked after 25 minutes by slipping a sharp knife between the backbone and the flesh. One should come away from the other with ease; if the flesh clings to the bones it needs a little longer.

Tip the juices into a bowl and stir in the capers. Fillet the salmon and serve with the caper butter spooned over.

Carbohydrate 2.2g Protein 61.7g

Salmon pie with minted courgettes

A fish pie is one of the great challenges for the low carb cook – they are potentially as high in fat and carbs as any dish can be, and make suitably luxurious eating. But equally, it is good to know that you can make a fab pie, reformed in its ways, and this one comes as a breath of fresh air – fish stew-like in its appeal with thin light juices. I would dish it up with a garlic mayonnaise, and a vegetable mash is also welcome. Because there is no potato or béchamel, it's also good eaten cold.

Serves 6

Salmon:
900g skinned salmon fillet,
    cut into 3–4cm pieces
100ml white wine
sea salt, black pepper

Sauce:
extra virgin olive oil
4 shallots, peeled and thinly sliced
2 garlic cloves, peeled and finely
    chopped
1 teaspoon finely chopped
    medium-hot red chilli
1 x 400g can chopped tomatoes
1 bay leaf
200g cooked and peeled prawns
100g pitted or stuffed green olives
a handful of fresh mint leaves,
    (about 10g)
800g courgettes, ends trimmed and
    finely sliced*
garlic mayonnaise, to serve

Place the salmon pieces in a large saucepan, pour over the wine and season with salt and pepper. Bring the liquid to the boil, then cover and cook over a medium–low heat for 4–5 minutes until the salmon is just cooked through – don't worry if a few patches still seem a little translucent. Reserving the liquor, remove the salmon using a slotted spoon, trying not to break it up, and transfer to a large bowl. Set aside while you make the sauce.

Heat a couple of tablespoons of oil in a medium saucepan over a medium heat and fry the shallots for a couple of minutes, stirring frequently, until translucent and starting to colour. Stir in the garlic and chilli and continue to fry momentarily until fragrant. Add the tomatoes and fish cooking liquor, including any given out by the salmon as it rests, the bay leaf and some seasoning. Bring to the boil, then cook over a low heat for 20–30 minutes until the sauce reduces to a thick purée and the oil separates out, stirring and keeping a watchful eye towards the end of this time.

Carefully spoon the salmon over the base of a 35cm oval gratin dish or one of equivalent size, discarding any additional liquid that has been released while it rested. Scatter the prawns and the olives over and between the salmon pieces. Discard the bay leaf and spoon the sauce over the fish, coating it as evenly as possible. You can prepare the pie to this point in advance, in which case allow it to cool, then cover and chill.

Preheat the oven to 190°C fan/210°C electric/gas 7. Whizz the mint to a purée with 4 tablespoons of the oil, then toss this with the courgettes and some seasoning in a large bowl, separating out the slices to evenly coat them. Arrange in an even layer to cover the fish, drizzle with another couple of tablespoons of oil and bake for 40–45 minutes until the top slices are patched with gold. Now heat the grill and pop the pie under to colour it further. Serve in shallow bowls, accompanied by garlic mayonnaise.
Carbohydrate 5.6g Protein 41.5g

---

*TIP: The quickest route here is to use the slicing attachment on a food processor.

Fish and chips with tartare sauce

Here we have homemade fish fingers, lightly coated in ground almonds in lieu of breadcrumbs, and oven-roasted chips that rely on celeriac rather than potato. You could get out the ketchup, but my own weakness is for tartare sauce.

This one's on my desert island list: just think of all those freshly caught fish cooked over an open fire – all you need for perfection is some mayonnaise laced with capers and gherkins.

Serves 4

Fish fingers:
100g ground almonds
1½ teaspoons sea salt
⅓ teaspoon cayenne pepper
1–2 medium eggs, beaten
400g skinned white fish fillets,
    1–2cm thick, cut into fingers
    2–3 wide and 5–7cm long
extra virgin olive oil
lemon wedges, to serve

Combine the ground almonds, salt and cayenne pepper in a shallow bowl, and put the egg in a second shallow bowl. Dip the fish fingers first into the egg and then into the ground almond mixture and set aside on a plate. Heat a couple of tablespoons of oil in a large, non-stick frying over a medium heat and fry the coated fish fingers in batches for about 2 minutes on the first side until golden, and for 1–2 minutes on the second side, scraping out any burnt crumbs between batches and replenishing the oil as necessary. Drain on a double thickness of kitchen paper, and serve with lemon wedges. You can also accompany them with chips and a teaspoon of tartare sauce, in which case a bowl of lettuce provides light relief.
Carbohydrate 1.5g Protein 22.3g

1.2kg celeriac, skin cut off
finely grated zest of 1 lemon
    (optional), plus 1 tablespoon
    lemon juice
2 tablespoons extra virgin olive oil
30g unsalted butter
sea salt, black pepper

WITH CELERIAC CHIPS
Preheat the oven to 200°C fan/220°C electric/gas 7. Slice the celeriac 1cm thick, then cut the slices into evenly sized chips – halve them if long. Arrange these in a large roasting dish (about 25 x 38cm) with the lemon zest if you like a particularly lemony flavour. Drizzle over the olive oil and the lemon juice and give the vegetables a stir. Dot with the butter, season and roast for 50–60 minutes, stirring the chips every 20 minutes by loosening them with a spatula.
Carbohydrate 8.7g Protein 26g

1 level teaspoon grainy mustard
1 level tablespoon finely chopped
    gherkins
1 level tablespoon finely chopped
    capers
1 heaped tablespoon finely chopped
    flat-leaf parsley
150g mayonnaise

WITH TARTARE SAUCE
I think pretty much everything tastes great with tartare sauce, it is lovely with the fishcakes on page 152 as well.

Stir all the ingredients together in a bowl, cover and chill until required.
Carbohydrate 9g Protein 26.2g

Prawn and pepper tagine

This tagine is light and delicate, with fresh ginger replacing the usual dried spices. And it is relatively dry, compared to many Moroccan stews, making it good for eating with vegetable accompaniments. I like to cook the prawns shell-on and peel them as I eat, but you could use raw peeled prawns if you prefer.

Serves 4

a large pinch of saffron filaments, (about 20)
4 red peppers
4 plum tomatoes
3 tablespoons extra virgin olive oil
450g unpeeled raw king prawns
4 garlic cloves, peeled and sliced
1 medium-hot red chilli, seeds and membranes discarded, and finely sliced
1 teaspoon finely grated fresh ginger
½ teaspoon tumeric
sea salt
a squeeze of lemon juice
4 tablespoons coarsely chopped coriander, to serve

Pour a tablespoon of boiling water over the saffron filaments in a small bowl and leave to infuse.

Preheat the oven to 200°C fan/220°C electric/gas 7 and roast the peppers on the oven rack for 15 minutes until the skin has blistered and started to colour. Remove them to a bowl, cover with clingfilm and leave to cool. Working over the bowl to reserve the juices, slip off the skins, remove the seeds and slice the flesh into thin strips.

Bring a small saucepan of water to the boil, cut out the cone from the top of each tomato, plunge into the boiling water for 20 seconds and then into a bowl of cold water. Remove and slip off the skins, and cut each tomato into 6–8 wedges.

Heat the olive oil in a large saucepan or cast-iron casserole over a medium–high heat, add the prawns and sauté on both sides until they turn from blue to pink. Transfer them to a bowl. Add the garlic, chilli and ginger to the pan and stir for about 30 seconds until nicely fragrant. Stir in the tumeric, add the tomatoes, and cook for a minute or two, mashing them down, then add the peppers, saffron water, pepper juices and some salt, cover and cook over a low heat for 10 minutes.

Give the sauce a stir, mashing the tomatoes to a coarse purée. Stir the prawns into the sauce, cover and cook for a further 5–6 minutes until the prawns feel firm when pressed. Season with a generous squeeze of lemon and taste for salt. Serve scattered with coriander.
Carbohydrate 13.5g Protein 12.3g

Poached trout with cucumber and dill sauce

Hugely under-rated, trout is a worthy alternative to salmon, and just as adaptable. If you want to serve it hot, allow the court-bouillon to cool, pour over the vinegared fish and place over a medium–high heat. The moment any bubbles present themselves on the surface, turn the heat down low and poach for 5 minutes. Here you could dress the trout with a fine drizzle of warm, melted salty butter, lemon juice, some sea salt and freshly ground black pepper. Hot or cold, I would serve the trout with watercress.

Serves 4

Court-bouillon:
2 carrots, trimmed, peeled and sliced
2 celery sticks, sliced
1 onion, peeled and chopped
1 bay leaf
a few parsley stalks
500ml white wine

Trout:
4 x trout (about 250g each), cleaned
150ml white wine vinegar
30g coarse sea salt

You will need to start preparing the trout several hours in advance of eating. Put the vegetables and herbs in a medium saucepan with the wine and 500ml water. Bring to the boil, cover and simmer over a low heat for 30 minutes.

Towards the end of this time, arrange the fish top to tail on their sides in a 30cm oval cast-iron casserole. Bring the vinegar to the boil in a small saucepan with the salt, stirring until it dissolves and pour evenly over the fish – any slime coating them should turn a greyish blue. Now pour the hot court-bouillon over the fish, bring it back to a healthy boil over a medium–high heat, then cover, remove from heat and leave to cool to blood temperature for several hours. Carefully lift the fish out of the court-bouillon on to plates to serve, dabbing any liquid that seeps out with kitchen paper.
Carbohydrate 11.5g Protein 36.3g

WITH CUCUMBER AND DILL SAUCE

Dill is particularly good with fish, and with cucumber, but should the fresh fronds prove hard to track down, chives would be next best.

2 tablespoons extra virgin olive oil
4 shallots, peeled and finely
    chopped
1 cucumber, peeled, quartered,
    deseeded and diced
sea salt, black pepper
4 tablespoons chopped dill, plus a
    little extra
300g zero-fat Greek yogurt
a squeeze of lemon juice

Heat the olive oil in a large frying pan over a medium heat and fry the shallots for 1–2 minutes, stirring occasionally, until softened without colouring. Add the cucumber, season and fry for a few minutes longer, again stirring occasionally. Transfer the vegetables to a bowl, stir in the dill and leave to cool. You can prepare the sauce to this point a couple of hours in advance. Shortly before serving, stir in the Greek yogurt and a squeeze of lemon juice, and taste for seasoning. Serve with the fish, scattering over a little extra dill.
Carbohydrate 16.2g Protein 44.7g

Fishcakes

A good fishcake is a suppertime staple, and these ones have passed the teenager litmus test. This involves the small white lie of not informing them it is celeriac instead of potato – and they didn't even suspect. Any fresh white fish fillets will be good here, but frequently frozen turn out fresher.

Serves 6

600g celeriac, skin cut off, cut
  into chunks
500g skinless white fish fillets,
  (cod, haddock, hake, etc)
100ml white wine
30g unsalted butter
sea salt, black pepper
1 teaspoon anchovy essence
  (optional)
2 tablespoons capers, rinsed and
  chopped
1 medium egg, beaten
12 rashers rindless streaky bacon
  (smoked or unsmoked)
a little groundnut oil

Bring a medium saucepan of salted water to the boil, add the celeriac and simmer for 15–20 minutes until tender. At the same time, arrange the fish fillets in a single layer on the base of another medium pan. Pour over the wine, dot with the butter and season them. Bring the wine to the boil, then cover the pan and cook over a low heat for 5–6 minutes. Transfer the fish to a plate using a spatula, and leave it to rest for 10 minutes.

Drain the celeriac into a sieve and leave for a few minutes to steam-dry and then reduce to a coarse purée in a food processor. Pour any juices given out by the fish back into the saucepan and reduce to a few tablespoons of buttery emulsion over a medium heat, then stir in the anchovy essence, if using. Flake the fish into a large bowl, discarding any bones, and mix in the mashed celeriac and capers. Mix in the cooking liquid, then the egg. Season the mixture to taste. Take heaped tablespoons of the mixture and form into 12 fishcakes, placing each one on top of a rasher of bacon, loosely bringing the ends up over the top (bearing in mind the bacon will contract as it cooks. You can prepare the fishcakes to this point up to a day in advance, in which case cover and chill them until required.

Preheat the oven to 200°C fan/220°C electric/gas 7. Arrange the fishcakes in a couple of roasting tins with the bacon ends on the base, drizzle over a little oil and bake for 30 minutes, carefully turning them halfway through.
Carbohydrate 3.4g Protein 23.8g

SIMPLY FISHCAKES
You can also pan-fry the fishcakes, leaving off the bacon. In this case shape them as 6 large or 12 small fishcakes and fry in a little **extra virgin olive oil** in a large, non-stick frying pan over a medium heat for about 4 minutes on the first side and 2–3 minutes on the second.
Carbohydrate 3.4g Protein 17.7g

WITH ROAST TOMATOES
Arrange 400–500g **cherry** or **small tomatoes on the vine** in a roasting dish so they fit snugly in a single layer. Drizzle over a tablespoon of **groundnut oil** and another of **balsamic vinegar**, and season them with **sea salt** and **black pepper**. Roast for 15 minutes at 200°C fan/220°C electric/gas 7, by which time the tomatoes will be soft and the skins will have burst.
Carbohydrate 6g Protein 18.3g

Chilli prawn stir-fry

With no heat to it, Sichuan pepper has little in common with our traditional fiery corns. Instead, it is an elegant, rust-red little pod scented with mint and lemongrass. First toasted and then ground and combined with salt it forms a classic seasoning within Sichuan cookery. Crisp deep-fried squid and prawns are restaurant favourites, though I prefer to pan-fry at home. For those who don't keep a well-stocked Oriental storecupboard, rapeseed oil provides just the right hint of nuts to take the place of sesame oil.

Serves 2

½ teaspoon Sichuan peppercorns
1 teaspoon sea salt
4 average heads of pak choi, base trimmed
2 tablespoons rapeseed or groundnut oil
1 teaspoon sesame oil (optional)
1 red onion, peeled and thinly sliced downwards into long strips
1 medium-hot red chilli, deseeded and cut into long thin strips
a splash of dark soy sauce
300g raw peeled king prawns, patted dry
1 large or 2 small spring onions, trimmed and cut into 6–8cm thin strips

Heat a small frying pan over a low heat, add the pepper and gently toast for a couple of minutes until fragrant, stirring now and again. Grind it in a pestle and mortar, then add the salt and combine.

Halve the heads of pak choi where the stalk meets the leaves and thinly slice lengthways into strips 5–9cm long. Heat a tablespoon of rapeseed or groundnut oil, with a teaspoon of sesame oil if you wish, in a large frying pan over a high heat. Add the onion and stir-fry for a minute or two until it begins to colour at the edges, then add the pak choi and chilli and fry for another couple of minutes until they start to wilt. Season with a splash of soy sauce and transfer to a serving plate. Add another tablespoon of oil to the pan and fry the prawns for a minute or two until pink and firm. Sprinkle over half the salt and pepper mixture, then mix the prawns into the pak choi. Scatter over the spring onion and serve with the rest of the salt and pepper for sprinkling over if wished.
Carbohydrate 8.6g Protein 29.3g

CHIPS

Chips £1
Fish in batter £3.50
Pies £2.50
Mushy peas £1

MASH, CHIPS OR ROAST?

Frequently the comfort we associate with the dishes we have grown up with has as much to do with the accompanying potatoes that go with them. It is the pile of buttery mash that comes with a slowly braised casserole of beef, the crispy roast potatoes that are *de rigueur* with our Sunday roast chicken, and of course chips with battered fish and tartare sauce, that induce that cathartic state of well-being. So I feel if we can crack this one then we're halfway there.

Letting other vegetables star in place of potatoes is something many chefs have been practising for years – think of that silky little turnip purée with a medallion of steak and wild mushrooms, or celeriac with a roast game bird. The only drawback is the no-holds-barred on the addition of butter and cream that rather undoes any potential health benefits.

So here I have tried to combine the best low carb alternatives to potatoes with healthy cooking methods and additions. I have never got the point of deep-fat fryers in a home kitchen (or deep-fried food), so no surprise that all the chips that follow are roasted, with just one exception of shallow-frying. And the mash, compared to the aforementioned restaurant version, is positively chaste.

MASH

Mash, in its traditional guise, is basically just a purée of potatoes, and we achieve different results depending on their variety and how we go about reducing them to a pulp. If the potatoes have been pressed through a mill then the mash should by rights be sublimely silky, whereas if it's been pounded with a retro masher, it is likely to be laced with alluring little nibs of potato.

And the guidelines for alternatives are pretty much the same. There are some vegetables, such as cauliflower, that are perhaps best 'mashed' in a food processor to leave them with a slight texture, while a fibrous vegetable like celeriac is most appealing if you reduce it to a purée in a liquidiser.

All mashes, I think, require something in the way of enriching, and in the recipes that follow I have suggested what I feel to be just enough, without going overboard. For instance, sour cream in lieu of crème fraîche (normally my default), which has a fraction of the fat, in fact about the same as single cream, which is basically little more than top of the milk. A very rich mash is fine every once in a while (like doughnuts, chocolate cake and croissants), but the idea here is food that you can eat without angst any day of the week you choose.

Also, like any potato mash, the purées can be flavoured at whim. One of my favourite ruses in recent years has been to make a herb purée pesto-style to spoon over the top and loosely fold into the mash to streak it. Make this with olive oil and it looks healthier by the second.

Carrot and swede mash

This has North European appeal, and as such is the ideal aside to many of the pies and casseroles in this book. These two vegetables marry together beautifully, and a little freshly grated nutmeg enhances their sweetness.

Serves 6

800g carrots, trimmed, peeled and
     cut into large chunks
800g swede, skin cut off and cut
     into even-sized chunks
75g unsalted butter, diced, plus a
     knob to serve
freshly grated nutmeg
sea salt, black pepper
milk

Bring a large pan of salted water to the boil, add the carrots and swede and cook for about 20 minutes or until tender, then drain into a sieve and leave for a few minutes for the surface moisture to evaporate. Purée the vegetables in a liquidiser with the butter, plenty of nutmeg, some seasoning and enough milk to loosen the mixture. Serve with a knob of butter and grinding of black pepper.
Carbohydrate 17.6g Protein 2g

ROOT VEG AND GINGER MASH
You can also scent the mash with fresh ginger, in which case liquidise it with 1 thick slice **fresh ginger root**, peeled and coarsely chopped.

Celeriac mash

Celeriac makes for one of the most characterful mashes, readily laced with mustard, when it's fab with red meat and guinea fowl. The only caveat is the difficulty sometimes of buying it. On the Continent, celeriac is as ubiquitous as potatoes, onions or garlic. Remoulade, the salad of grated celeriac dressed with a mustard mayonnaise, is French for coleslaw, and it also makes its appearance as a purée, in *'pot au…'* pretty much everything, and as chips too. So its scarcity is purely a cultural division. These days I buy up several roots at a time and keep them as a standby.

Serves 6

a slug of vinegar, (white wine or cider)
1.5kg celeriac, skin cut off, and cut into chunks
50g salted butter, diced, plus a knob to serve
sea salt, black pepper
freshly grated nutmeg
milk

Bring a large pan of water to the boil and acidulate it with a slug of vinegar. Add the celeriac and simmer for 20–30 minutes until tender. Drain into a colander and leave for a few minutes to steam dry.

Purée the celeriac with the butter, some salt, pepper and nutmeg in a liquidiser, adding enough milk to kickstart the process and achieve a purée. You'll probably need to do this in batches. Transfer to a serving dish, reheating it first if necessary, and drop a knob of butter in the centre.
Carbohydrate 6.3g Protein 3.3g

CELERIAC AND MUSTARD MASH
Stir a teaspoon each of **Dijon** and **grainy mustard** into the finished mash.
Carbohydrate 6.4g Protein 3.4g

Brussels sprout and parsley mash

Try out this one on sprout sceptics because, like cauliflower, I think so often it is the texture of this vegetable that some find offputting. Turned into a luscious green mash with sour cream, flat-leaf parsley and a few drops of red wine vinegar and it is unrecognisable.

Serves 6

900g Brussels sprouts, bottoms trimmed and outer leaves removed
2 scant teaspoons red wine vinegar
150g sour cream
4 tablespoons coarsely chopped flat-leaf parsley
sea salt, black pepper
a knob of salted butter, to serve

Bring a large pan of salted water to the boil, add the sprouts and simmer for 15–20 minutes until tender. Drain them into a colander and leave for a minute or two for any excess water to evaporate. Place them in the bowl of a food processor with the vinegar, sour cream, parsley and some seasoning and whizz to a smooth purée. Return the purée to the saucepan, and gently reheat when required. Serve with a knob of butter dropped into the centre.
Carbohydrate 7.4g Protein 6.1g

Broccoli mash

The large flowering heads of broccoli have come to look like a poor relation in proximity to sexier long-stemmed varieties. But here it is the old-fashioned type that we are after (incidentally, these heads are also best for making soups).

Serves 6

900g broccoli florets (trimmed weight)
50g salted butter, diced
4 tablespoons extra virgin olive oil, plus extra to serve
sea salt, black pepper

Bring a large pan of salted water to the boil and simmer the broccoli florets for about 15 minutes until really soft. Drain the broccoli in a colander, shaking it thoroughly, and reduce to a textured purée in a food processor with the butter, olive oil and some seasoning. Transfer to a serving dish and pour over a little extra oil.
Carbohydrate 2.9g Protein 6.7g

BROCCOLI AND PARSLEY MASH
Whizz the broccoli with 25g **flat-leaf parsley** to coarsely chop it for a really lively, vibrant mash, and scatter over a little extra chopped when serving.

Cauliflower mash

Cauliflower has a delicacy and elegance that comes to the fore when it is puréed. I think it benefits from a slight rusticity of texture, but you can also make a smooth purée by whizzing it in a liquidiser with enough milk to achieve the right consistency, and this makes a *soignée* base for all manner of delicate fish, some grilled lamb chops or a rare steak.

Serves 6

1kg cauliflower florets (about 2 cauliflowers)
150g sour cream
sea salt, black pepper
freshly grated nutmeg
knob of salted butter, to serve

Bring a large pan of salted water to the boil, add the cauliflower and cook for about 15 minutes until tender. Drain in a colander, leave for a few minutes to steam dry then whizz to a purée in a food processor with the sour cream, some seasoning and nutmeg. You may need to do this in batches. This can be made in advance and gently reheated. Transfer to a serving dish, grate over a little more nutmeg and drop a knob of butter in the centre.
Carbohydrate 6.2g Protein 6.8g

CAULIFLOWER AND PESTO MASH
Make the purée as above with 100g **sour cream** and omit the nutmeg. Whizz 20g **basil leaves**, 3 tablespoons **extra virgin olive oil**, a squeeze of **lemon juice** and a little **sea salt** to a textured purée in a food processor. Transfer the mash to a serving dish, spoon the purée on top and fold over a few times until streaked with green. You can also scatter over a few more tiny basil leaves.
Carbohydrate 12g Protein 13.4g

ABOVE: *Roast pumpkin and tomato mash*

Two pumpkin mashes

My local greengrocer stocks big, French buff-coloured pumpkins with a really dark orange aromatic flesh (the variety remains a mystery), and they do make a fab mash. Do try for one of the heirloom varieties such as Crown Prince, or ones that are grown with the table in mind rather than those intended to be carved into Halloween lanterns, which can have only a thin layer of flesh.

ROAST PUMPKIN AND TOMATO MASH

Roasting any vegetable will concentrate its flavour as the juices are driven off and sugars caramelise, and given that pumpkin can be on the tame side, it's an ideal way of cooking it. This particular mash is sharpened with tomatoes and roast garlic, so it goes hand in hand with other Mediterranean flavours.

Serves 6

1kg pumpkin flesh (about 1.5kg
    whole), cut into chunks
300g small tomatoes
4 garlic cloves, unpeeled
extra virgin olive oil
sea salt, black pepper
finely chopped flat-leaf parsley,
    to serve

Preheat the oven to 200°C fan/220°C electric/gas 7. Arrange the pumpkin, tomatoes and garlic in a roasting dish. Drizzle over 4 tablespoons of oil and season. Roast for 50 minutes, until softened and starting to colour. Leave for about 10 minutes to cool a little, then slip the skins off the tomatoes (you can wear rubber gloves for this), and squeeze out the insides of the garlic. Purée the contents of the roasting dish in a food processor. Taste for seasoning and reheat if necessary, though it is still good warm. Serve drizzled with oil and scattered with parsley.
Carbohydrate 5.7g Protein 1.7g

PUMPKIN AND APPLE MASH

This wintery pumpkin and apple mash is a natural with any meaty bangers. Look out for French sausages such as Toulouse: if they are the genuine article they shouldn't contain any bread. Merguez, typically North African sausages, are also worth researching.

Serves 4

50g unsalted butter
1.2kg pumpkin flesh (about 1.8kg
    whole), coarsely diced
3 eating apples, peeled, cored and
    coarsely diced
50ml orange juice
sea salt, black pepper
2 tablespoons extra virgin olive oil
a generous squeeze of lemon juice
4 tablespoons snipped chives

Melt the butter in a large saucepan over a medium heat and fry the pumpkin and apple for about 5 minutes, stirring frequently. Add the orange juice and plenty of seasoning, cover and cook over a low heat for 15 minutes. Drain off the liquid, and coarsely mash the pumpkin and apple using a potato masher, then stir in the olive oil, a squeeze of lemon juice and the chives, and taste for seasoning.
Carbohydrate 18.1g Protein 2.8g

Spring root mash

Each of these spring roots provides a different texture, the end result is a delicious mélange of the best of the vegetable patch at that time of year.

Serves 6

50g unsalted butter, plus a knob
   to serve
sea salt, black pepper
400g small turnips, trimmed,
   peeled and halved if necessary
400g slim carrots, trimmed, peeled
   and thickly sliced diagonally
400g slim leeks (trimmed weight),
   thickly sliced diagonally
1 tablespoon extra virgin olive oil
freshly grated nutmeg
finely chopped chives, to serve

Bring 600ml water to the boil with the butter and a teaspoon of salt in a medium–large saucepan. Add the turnips and carrots, bring the liquid back to the boil, cover and cook over a medium–low heat for 8 minutes, stirring in the leeks after 2 minutes.

Drain and whizz the contents to a purée in a food processor with the olive oil and a grating of nutmeg, then season to taste. Transfer to a serving dish, drop in a knob of butter and scatter with chives.

CHIPS

I confess I've never been very big on chips. I adore the skinny fries that we get in France, but I can pass on most others. As for frozen oven-cooked chips, why, when there are so many other wonderful alternative vegetable options, go for second best? So the recipes that follow are in my eyes an improvement, even though they are altogether different, and I realise I may have some problem convincing the diehards out there to switch camps.

I am inclined to think that a large part of what we love about chips is their shape and the sensation of eating them. I also prize that light crunch of fine sea salt crystals scrunched over at the end, and we can still have that. We can also have the fish, the burgers and the sausages we love to eat with them. And the ketchup and tartare sauce.

Chunky celeriac chips

These are particularly good with beef, as are swede chips, a vegetable that is horribly overlooked, though I do realise it is not to everyone's taste, while celeriac has more universal appeal, perhaps its association with remoulade gives it a head start.

Serves 4

1.6kg celeriac, skin cut off and
    sliced into wedges 1–2cm thick
100g unsalted butter
sea salt
paprika or piment
    d'espelette (optional)

Preheat the oven to 190°C fan/210°C electric/gas 7. Arrange the celeriac in a large roasting dish that will hold it in a crowded single layer. Clarify the butter by gently melting it in a small saucepan, skim off the surface foam and pour the clear liquid over the celeriac, season with salt and toss to coat it. Roast for 1–1¼ hours, turning with a spatula halfway through. Season with a little paprika or piment d'espelette if wished.
Carbohydrate 8.6g Protein 4.6g

Courgette chips

We have a local burger bar that keeps every member of the family happy, with triple-topped burgers and ice-cream smoothies for teenagers, and skinny burgers (ie without a bun), and courgette fries for the likes of myself.

Serves 4

1 medium egg
1 tablespoon extra virgin olive oil
sea salt
paprika
800g courgettes, ends trimmed, and cut into chips 1cm diameter and 5–7cm long

Whisk the egg with the olive oil, 1 tablespoon of still or fizzy water, some salt and paprika in a large bowl. Toss the courgette chips with the egg mixture to very lightly coat them. On removing them from the bowl, use a slotted utensil so that any excess egg mixture is left behind.

OVEN-ROASTED
Before dipping the courgettes, preheat the oven to 230°C fan/250°C electric/gas 9 and use a pastry brush to lightly coat the base of a couple of roasting dishes with a thin film of olive oil. Scatter the dipped chips over the base of the dishes in a single layer, and roast for 25–30 minutes until golden, turning them with a spatula halfway through. A lower tray will probably take longer than one on top.
Carbohydrate 3.7g Protein 5.2g

FRIED
Heat about 1cm of **vegetable oil** in a large frying pan over a medium heat until a drop of the egg mixture sizzles when added. Fry the chips in batches for a few minutes, turning them halfway, until golden and crispy. Remove with a slotted spoon and drain on kitchen paper; stack in a bowl, scrunching over some sea salt.
Carbohydrate 3.7g Protein 5.2g

Thick-cut pumpkin chips

I adore these pumpkin chips, roasting does them a huge favour and they turn deliciously caramelised.

Serves 4

600g pumpkin flesh, (about 1kg whole)
2 tablespoons extra virgin olive oil, plus extra for oiling
2 tablespoons fresh lemon thyme leaves
sea salt

Preheat the oven to 190°C fan/210°C electric/gas 7. Cut the pumpkin into chunky chips roughly 3cm in diameter and toss in a large bowl with the olive oil and thyme. Brush the base of a large roasting tin with oil and spread the chips out in a crowded single layer. Roast for 40–45 minutes, carefully turning them halfway through using a spatula. Scrunch over some sea salt, and carefully turn to season them on the other side, then transfer to a bowl to serve.
Carbohydrate 3.7g Protein 1.1g

ROAST

Roasted and grilled veg have a luxurious quality when cooked with olive oil. And they will take the place of starchier offerings like potatoes and parsnips when you are after a traditional line-up.

Roast peppers

These are particularly good once the barbecue season is upon us.

Serves 6

6 red or orange peppers, core, seeds and membranes removed
8–10 fresh thyme sprigs
2 bay leaves
5 garlic cloves, peeled and sliced
4 tablespoons extra virgin olive oil
sea salt, black pepper
1 teaspoon balsamic vinegar

Preheat the oven to 180°C fan/200°C electric/gas 6. Quarter the peppers and arrange in a crowded single layer in a baking dish or roasting pan. Tuck in the herbs and scatter over the garlic. Drizzle over the oil and season with salt and pepper.

Roast for 45–50 minutes, stirring and basting at least twice to ensure the peppers emerge succulent and evenly singed at the edges. Remove from the oven, drip the vinegar over and vaguely stir to mix it into the juices. Leave to cool.
Carbohydrate 10.5g Protein 1.8g

Dish up with a selection of *hors d'oeuvres* – **green** and **black olives**, **salami**, **gherkins** and **caper berries**.
Carbohydrate 10.7g Protein 3.7g

Crispy roast onions

An alternative to fried onion rings – healthier and easier to cook.

Serves 6

900g red onions, peeled, halved and sliced
extra virgin olive or vegetable oil
1 teaspoon red wine vinegar
sea salt

Preheat the oven to 170°C fan/190°C electric/gas 5. Spread out the onions in a thin layer on two baking sheets, breaking the slices into rings as far as possible. Drizzle over a little oil and roast for 35 minutes, stirring halfway through to ensure they caramelise evenly. Remove from the oven, transfer to a bowl, and toss with a teaspoon of vinegar and some salt. Serve warm or at room temperature.
Carbohydrate 12g Protein 1.8g

Char-grilled courgettes

Another great basic that you can cook well in advance that makes for relaxed grazing with all the usual Mediterranean goodies like sun-dried tomatoes, olives and Parma ham. And you can also build them into a salad, or serve them very simply with some roast chicken or chops.

Serves 6

4 courgettes, ends removed,
    cut into long thin strips
extra virgin olive oil
sea salt, black pepper

Heat a ridged cast-iron griddle over a medium–high heat, brush one side of as many courgette slices as will fit with olive oil, season and grill this side for 3–5 minutes until striped with gold, then brush the top side, turn and grill this side too. Remove them to a plate and grill the remainder in the same fashion, then leave the slices to cool. You can cook them well in advance.
Carbohydrate 3.5g Protein 2.3g

AS A SALAD WITH OLIVES
Shortly before eating, scatter 3 **spring onions**, trimmed and thinly sliced diagonally, and 75g pitted **black olives** over the courgettes, drizzle over a little more oil and dust with **paprika**.
Carbohydrate 3.7g Protein 2.5g

Roast carrot wedges

This turns a humble root into a star of a dish. Good with a roast, you can leave them to cool a little and toss them into a pile of salad leaves with some crispy bacon or ham. You want good-sized roots, not real brutes, but not tiddlers either – they will only shrivel up on cooking.

Serves 6

4 tablespoons extra virgin olive oil
1kg chunky carrots, trimmed,
    peeled, halved or quartered
    lengthways, and halved into
    2 shorter lengths
1 large onion, peeled and cut into
    thin wedges
several bay leaves
1 head of garlic, broken into cloves
sea salt, black pepper

Preheat the oven to 190°C fan/210°C electric/gas 7. Heat 2 tablespoons of olive oil over a high heat in a large heavy-duty roasting dish (about 25 x 38cm) on the hob. Add the carrots and fry for about 10 minutes, stirring frequently, until well on the way to being coloured, adding the onion halfway through. This gives the veggies a head start before their roasting. Now toss in the bay leaves and garlic, season generously, drizzle over another couple of tablespoons of oil and roast for 40–50 minutes until golden on the outside and soft within, stirring halfway through. The insides of the garlic cloves can be squeezed out and eaten.
Carbohydrate 17.1g Protein 1.9g

Grilled aubergine

These thick slices are delicately caramelised on the outside and meltingly creamy within. Endlessly versatile, you can eat them with anything and everything.

Serves 6

3 aubergines, ends discarded,
    cut into 1–2cm slices
extra virgin olive oil
sea salt, black pepper

Preheat the oven to 190°C fan/210°C electric/gas 7. Lay the aubergine out on a couple of baking trays, brushing the slices with oil on both sides, and seasoning the top. Roast for 20 minutes, then turn them and cook for a further 10–20 minutes until golden; the lower tray may need longer than the top. Loosen with a spatula and serve hot or cold.
Carbohydrate 3.5g Protein 1.4g

AS A SALAD
Lay the slices out on a large platter, dollop each one with **Greek yogurt**, scatter with **pomegranate seeds** and coarsely chopped **coriander** or **flat-leaf parsley**.
Carbohydrate 6.9g Protein 4.1g

Roasted roots

This offers a gorgeous blast of colour and flavour, great with any roast, including fish. And, like most roast vegetables, they are good for grazing on at room temperature.

Serves 4

500g celeriac, skin cut off and
    sliced into wedges 1–2cm thick
400g beetroot, tops and tails
    trimmed, cut into wedges
400g carrots, halved lengthways
    and cut into two shorter lengths
75g unsalted butter
sea salt, black pepper

Preheat the oven to 190°C fan/210°C electric/gas 7. Arrange the vegetables in a large roasting dish that will hold them in a crowded single layer. Clarify the butter by gently melting it in a small saucepan, skim off the surface foam and pour the clear liquid over the vegetables, discarding the milky solids below. Season with salt and pepper and toss to coat. Roast for 70–75 minutes until golden, turning with a spatula halfway through.
Carbohydrate 18.5g Protein 3.9g

WITH PERSILLADE
Sprinkle the roast veg with persillade and serve them with air-dried ham and olives.

Make a persillade by whizzing 20g **flat-leaf parsley** and 2 peeled **garlic cloves** in a food processor until very finely chopped. Scatter over the vegetables and serve.
Carbohydrate 19.5g Protein 10.4g

ABOVE: *Roasted roots (see page 169)*

ABOVE: *Roasted roots with Persillade (see page 169)*

OTHER LOVELY VEGGIES

This is a *mélange* of vegetable dishes that don't quite fit 'mash, chips or roast', or salad, but look beyond steamed or lightly blanched. And there is nothing wrong with either of those ways of preparation, especially if there is a sauce or some juice to dress them. But we start with a few dishes, cooked with a minimum of fuss, broccoli for instance, that can be griddled, smothered or sautéed and cabbages in endless guises. We might not want them in 'Miracle Soups' but I grow even fonder of these vegetables with every year that passes.

There are a handful of stand-ins: a rösti, made with root vegetables that are deliciously crispy around the edges; an oven-baked bubble and squeak, where swede stars in the place of potatoes; and the aptly named spaghetti squash. When it's in season this is about as close as

nature gets to providing a plate of noodles. In addition to dressing it with the garlic butter suggested here, the method of cooking it will provide the foundation for any number of other ways you might want to serve it. And, finally, there are a few composite vegetable dishes, ones that will stand on their own, or at least with precious little aside.

Green beans with smoky bacon

I still regard green beans, or *haricots verts*, when they are as skinny as a reed and very lightly cooked and tossed with a knob of salty Normandy butter, as conceivably the ultimate in vegetable luxury. So it is only one step on to combine them with silky whole shallots and crispy lardons. Serve these with a roast, or equally with an egg, poached or fried and there is no need to elaborate any further.

Serves 4

30g salted butter
½ teaspoon sea salt
250g small shallots, peeled
150g rindless smoked back bacon, sliced
350g fine green beans, topped and tailed

Heat the butter in a small saucepan with the salt and 2 tablespoons of water until simmering. Add the whole peeled shallots, cover and cook over a low heat for 15 minutes by which time they should be tender and sitting in a buttery sauce, the water having evaporated.

At the same time heat a large non-stick frying pan over a medium heat, add the bacon and fry for 8–12 minutes until golden and crisp, stirring now and again. Drain the bacon on a double thickness of kitchen paper and leave to cool. You can prepare the onions and bacon to this point in advance.

Bring a large pan of salted water to the boil, add the beans and simmer for 3–5 minutes until just tender. Drain them into a colander and leave for a moment for the surface water to evaporate. Gently reheat the onions then toss in the hot beans, coating them with the butter, and then the bacon.
Carbohydrate 4.9g Protein 9.8g

Duo of brassicas

Cauliflower is a little like potato in that it struggles to find its voice without a supporting cast. So combining it with broccoli, which has a sufficiently different character, creates interest.

Serves 4

4 tablespoons extra virgin olive oil
3 garlic cloves, peeled and thinly sliced
½ teaspoon sea salt, eg Maldon
300g cauliflower florets (3–4cm)
300g tender-stem broccoli (trimmed weight), halved lengthways

Put 400ml water in a medium saucepan with the olive oil, garlic and salt and bring to the boil. Add the cauliflower, bring the liquid back to the boil, cover and cook over a medium–low heat for 10 minutes, stirring in the broccoli after 4 minutes, then drain off the liquid.
Carbohydrate 2.3g Protein 2.7g

Broccoli three ways - grilled/sautéed/steamed

There is less waste with long-stem broccolis than the standard, they are more like asparagus in that you can eat most of the stalk down to where it becomes visibly tough or pale in colour. Tenderstem broccoli may have a little less flavour than purple sprouting, but it is true to its name by comparison – purple sprouting can be hit and miss, and on the stringy side, even after you've peeled the stalk. I also particularly like the texture of the heads of tenderstem, but either is a treat.

PURPLE SPROUTING
Cut the stalks off the broccoli so that you are left with the flowering head, a few small leaves and buds, about 7–8cm long, and reserve the stalks for soup. Alternatively you can cut them that much longer, about 12cm, and peel to just below the base.

TENDERSTEM
Trim the stalks accordingly – you may see other buds or leaves have been trimmed off at this junction. Being relatively thin, there is no great merit in peeling them.

Serves 4

400g long-stem broccoli, stems trimmed
extra virgin olive oil
sea salt, black pepper

Serves 4

4 tablespoons extra virgin olive oil
400g long-stem broccoli, trimmed
sea salt, black pepper

Serves 6

800g purple-sprouting broccoli, trimmed
50g butter
sea salt, black pepper

GRILLED
Bring a large saucepan of salted water to the boil. Add the broccoli to the boiling water, pushing it well down, and cook for 3 minutes, then drain into a colander and leave for a few minutes to steam-dry.

Heat a griddle over a medium heat. Toss the broccoli in a large bowl with oil to coat it and season. Grill in batches for about 2 minutes on either side until patched with gold. It can be served hot or cold.
Carbohydrate 2.7g Protein 3.3g

SAUTÉED
Heat a couple of tablespoons of oil in a large frying pan over a medium heat. Add half the broccoli, season and fry for 3–4 minutes until coloured, turning halfway through. Add a generous splash of water to the pan, clamp on a lid and cook for about 5 minutes over a lowish heat until the thickest parts of the stalks are tender. Remove this to a plate (you can cover it with foil to keep it warm), and cook the other half in the same way.
Carbohydrate 2.7g Protein 3.3g

STEAMED
Give the flowering heads a good rinse in a colander, then place in a large saucepan with 4 tablespoons water, dot with the butter and season. Cover and cook over a medium heat for about 15 minutes until tender, stirring halfway through.
Carbohydrate 3.7g Protein 5.3g

Cavolo nero with anchovies, chilli and garlic

For some years after this vegetable appeared I was still looking over the shoulders of the fans gathering around it, wondering what all the fuss was about. And then realisation dawned, or rather I tried dressing it with olive oil, lemon juice, anchovies and chilli, and cupid's arrow struck.

Serves 4

sea salt
about 600g cavolo nero
5 tablespoons extra virgin olive oil
4 garlic cloves, peeled and finely chopped
1 tablespoon finely chopped medium-hot red chilli (seeds discarded)
12 salted anchovy fillets, sliced across
2 tablespoons lemon juice

Bring a large saucepan two-thirds full with salted water to the boil. Cut the cavolo nero leaves off the thin central stalk (even the finest sections at the tip will be tough if left) and then thickly slice the leaves across.

Add the leaves to the pan and cook for 3 minutes, pushing them down now and again so they cook evenly. At the same time, heat a tablespoon of oil in a non-stick frying pan over a medium heat, add the garlic and chilli and cook briefly, stirring frequently, until the garlic is sizzling and just starting to colour, then remove from the heat and stir in the anchovies to warm through, followed by the lemon juice and a further 2 tablespoons of oil.

Drain the cavolo nero into a colander and press out the excess water using the back of a wooden spoon or a potato masher, return to the pan and toss with a couple of tablespoons of oil. Transfer this to a serving plate and drizzle over the contents of the frying pan.
Carbohydrate 3g Protein 8.5g

Buttery spring roots

This is the root equivalent of Duo of brassicas (see page 174), and the same goes for amassing several different vegetables together: they are all the more lavish than dished up on their own.

Serves 4

25g unsalted butter
½ teaspoon sea salt, eg Maldon
½ teaspoon caster sugar
200g small turnips, trimmed, peeled and halved if necessary
200g slim carrots, trimmed, peeled and thickly sliced diagonally
200g slim leeks (trimmed weight), thickly sliced diagonally

Bring 300ml water to the boil with the butter, salt and sugar in a medium–large saucepan. Add the turnips and carrots, bring the liquid back to the boil, cover and cook over a medium–low heat for 8 minutes, stirring in the leeks after 2 minutes, then drain off the liquid.
Carbohydrate 7.1g Protein 1.6g

Crispy cabbage gratin

Of the many vegetables of which I am the sole member of the Appreciation Society (within my own family), none is met with greater disdain than Brussels sprouts. I adore sprouts, but for the most part we all save them for a once-a-year Christmas blow-out, and even then curse them for the time they take to trim and the fact they exist at all.

Sprouts have a sophisticated edge, easy enough to see why children might not take to the curious bitterness that defines them, but I would put them in the same league as Stilton, Angostura Bitters and Marmite, all of which are tastes worth acquiring.

If there is any justification to hating them, then surely it has to do with their being boiled. Two ways around this are either to cook and purée, or sauté them, especially with a bit of bacon. But it was revelation to discover one idle suppertime that they actually roast up a treat too. So if you happen to be one of those doubters, do give this one a go.

Serves 6

1–1½ sweetheart or pointed cabbage (about 600g), base trimmed, outer leaves discarded
500g Brussels sprouts, base trimmed, outer leaves discarded and halved downwards
1 red onion, peeled, halved and thinly sliced
4 tablespoons extra virgin olive oil
sea salt, black pepper

Preheat the oven to 190°C fan/210°C electric/gas 7. Cut the sweetheart cabbage into thin wedges, leaving them attached by the thick central stalk at the base, then cut in half any sections longer than about 10cm. Arrange the cabbage, Brussels and the red onion in a large roasting dish (about 25 x 38cm), drizzle over the olive oil, season and toss to coat everything. Roast for about 40 minutes, stirring every 15 minutes, until golden and crispy at the edges.
Carbohydrate 8.9g Protein 4.8g

Savoy cabbage with caraway

There is no accompaniment that suits a slowly roasted joint quite like a big bowl of cabbage. And of all the varieties, Savoy has to be the first choice. Both caraway and chilli bring out the best in cabbage, but it's as well to exercise a cautious hand – a little of both spices goes a long way.

Serves 4

1 Savoy cabbage, base trimmed, outer leaves discarded
⅓ teaspoon caraway seeds
2 tablespoons extra virgin olive oil
a small pinch of dried chilli flakes
sea salt

Quarter the cabbage and cut out the core, then finely slice the leaves (as they are so tightly packed I tend not to bother to wash them). Lightly pound the caraway seeds in a pestle and mortar to break them up. Heat the oil in a large saucepan over a medium heat, add the caraway and chilli and give it a stir, then add the cabbage, season with salt and stir-fry for a couple of minutes until it is glossy. Add 3 tablespoons of water, clamp on a lid and cook over a low heat for 15 minutes, or until the toughest parts are tender, stirring halfway through. The cabbage is quite good natured, and can be reheated if wished. Any leftover makes a delicious bubble and squeak (see page 182).
Carbohydrate 8g Protein 4.3g

WHITE CABBAGE WITH NUTMEG
Discarding any damaged outer leaves, quarter a **white cabbage**, cut out the core and slice wafer-fine into strands 5–7 cm long. Melt 30g **unsalted butter** in a large saucepan over a medium–low heat, add the cabbage, season with **sea salt**, **black pepper** and a generous grating of **nutmeg** and fry for 5–10 minutes, stirring frequently, until relaxed and lightly coloured.
Carbohydrate 7.9g Protein 2.2g

Swiss chard with coriander, allspice and pomegranate

Like so many cabbages, Swiss chard greets spices and fruits like old friends – they get on very well together, and any potential austerity is further softened by a mass of golden fried onions and a generous addition of coriander.

Serves 6

3 tablespoons extra virgin olive oil
2 large onions, peeled, halved and finely sliced across
a slug of vinegar, (white wine or cider)
500–600g Swiss chard
½ teaspoon allspice
sea salt
30g coriander leaves, coarsely chopped
sumac (optional)
3 heaped tablespoons pomegranate seeds

Heat 2 tablespoons of oil in a large saucepan over a medium heat and fry the onions for 15–20 minutes, stirring frequently, until creamy and golden.

At the same time bring a large saucepan of water to the boil and acidulate it with a slug of vinegar. Cut the chard leaves off the stalks and thickly slice them, then thinly slice the stalks. Add the stalks to the pan and cook for 5 minutes, then add the leaves and cook for a further 2 minutes. Drain into a colander and shake dry.

Stir the allspice into the onions, and then add the chard. Season with salt and gently fry for a couple of minutes to acquaint the ingredients, then stir in the coriander. Transfer to a serving dish, drizzle over the remaining tablespoon of oil, scatter over some sumac if wished and then the pomegranate seeds.
Carbohydrate 9.6g Protein 2.6g

Oven-baked bubble and squeak

This bubble, cooked in the oven, is easier than hovering over a frying pan, enjoyable as that process is. It also has a sense of being heartier, or more in line with a pie, but with the same potential as classic bubble as an aside to any of the casseroles, or on its own with poached or fried eggs, grilled tomatoes and mushrooms. And crispy bacon.

Serves 6

1.5kg swede, skin cut off and cut
    into even-sized chunks
2 tablespoons groundnut or
    vegetable oil
50g unsalted butter
1 onion, peeled and finely chopped
200–250g Savoy cabbage, outer
    leaves discarded, tough stalks
    removed and coarsely chopped
sea salt, black pepper
1 heaped teaspoon grainy mustard
a couple of handfuls of coarsely
    chopped flat-leaf parsley

Bring a large saucepan of salted water to the boil, add the swede and cook for 20–30 minutes until tender, then drain into a colander, return to the pan and coarsely mash using a potato masher. Press out the excess liquid from the swede in a sieve in batches, again using a potato masher, and transfer to a large bowl.

Heat a tablespoon of oil and half the butter in a large frying pan over a medium heat, add the onion and fry for a few minutes, stirring occasionally, until glossy and starting to colour, then add the cabbage and fry for a couple of minutes longer, turning constantly, until it relaxes. Combine the onion and cabbage with the swede, season generously and stir in the mustard and the parsley. You can prepare the bubble to this point in advance, in which case leave to cool, cover and chill.

Preheat the oven to 200°C fan/220°C electric/gas 7. Drizzle a tablespoon of oil over the base of a cast-iron or other roasting dish (about 20 x 30cm) and place in the oven for 10 minutes. Press the swede mixture into the hot pan, leaving the surface on the rough side. Dot with the remaining butter and bake for 35–40 minutes until golden at the tips and around the edge.
Carbohydrate 15.8g Protein 3g

Spaghetti squash with garlic butter

These fairly rare buff-coloured squashes are marrow-like in size and appearance. Would we saw more of them. I recall being surprised, charmed and amazed the very first time I cut one open and forked its flesh into fine spaghetti-like strands, hence the name. They merit any pasta or noodle-like treatment, here slightly decadently with garlic butter and Parmesan, but add this to your personal taste.

Serves 4

Spaghetti squash:
1 x 1.8kg spaghetti squash
freshly grated Parmesan to serve
(optional)

Garlic butter:
100g unsalted butter, softened
2 garlic cloves, peeled and coarsely
chopped
zest of 1 lemon, plus a generous
squeeze of juice
sea salt, black pepper
3 tablespoons finely chopped
flat-leaf parsley
2 tablespoons finely chopped chives

You either want a large preserving pan (or cast-iron oval casserole) to cook the squash, or failing that, if it is too long for your biggest saucepan, simply cut off the stalk end to fit. Half-fill the pan with water and bring to the boil. Prick the squash all over with a skewer. Add to the pan, cover and simmer over a low heat for 40 minutes or until tender when pierced with a knife, turning it over halfway through.

In the meantime place the butter, garlic, lemon zest and juice, and some seasoning in the bowl of a food processor and blend at high speed until creamy and amalgamated. Add the chopped herbs and give another quick whizz to incorporate them. This can also be made well in advance.

Remove the squash from the pan, slice in half lengthways and scoop out the seeds, then fork the flesh into a large bowl into long spaghetti strands. Tip this into a sieve, set it back over the bowl, and press out the excess liquid using a potato masher. Transfer the spaghetti strands to a shallow serving dish and fork to separate the lump a little. Half melt the garlic butter in a small saucepan and pour this over, cutting through the squash a few times to roughly mix it in. Serve with freshly grated Parmesan if wished.
Carbohydrate 16.3g Protein 2.5g

Leek, chicory and Parma ham bake

Both leeks and chicory turn delectably succulent when braised, one is sweet, the other slightly bitter, and the Parma ham salty – a perfect storm. As well as being lovely on its own, this will lend its hand as an aside to roast chicken, or for eating cold with a sheep's cheese.

Serves 4

500–600g leeks (trimmed weight), halved lengthways
3 garlic cloves, peeled and cut into 2–3 slivers
200ml white wine
6 tablespoons extra virgin olive oil
1 tablespoon soft thyme leaves
sea salt, black pepper
4 heads of chicory, base trimmed, outer leaves discarded and halved lengthways
1 tablespoon white wine vinegar
8 slices Parma ham
coarsely chopped flat-leaf parsley (optional)

Preheat the oven to 160°C fan/180°C electric/gas 4. Arrange the leeks, cut-side up, lengthways in a crowded single layer in a suitable roasting dish (about 20 x 30cm), overlapping as necessary and tucking the garlic in between. Pour over the wine and drizzle over 3 tablespoons of oil. Scatter over the thyme and season. Toss the chicory with a couple of tablespoons of oil and the vinegar in a large bowl and arrange, cut-side down, on top of the leeks, so they lie lengthways in the same fashion, and season them. Cover with foil and bake for 1 hour.

Turn up the oven temperature to 200°C fan/220°C electric/gas 7. Uncover the gratin, baste the vegetables with the juices, then drape a slice of ham along each half of chicory (this will shrink as it cooks). Drizzle over another tablespoon of oil and return to the oven for 20 minutes or until the ham is golden and crisp. Serve hot or at room temperature with the juices drizzled over, scattered with parsley if wished.
Carbohydrate 9.6g Protein 9.4g

Root veg and apple gratin

This will take the place of potatoes with a joint of roast pork or lamb, and you can also use swede in lieu of celeriac. Try to slice the vegetables as thinly as possible to avoid gaps when you layer them, a task that is best done by hand.

Serves 6

600g celeriac, skin cut off, cut downwards into wedges and finely sliced
600g carrots, trimmed, peeled and finely sliced
4 tablespoons extra virgin olive oil
2 garlic cloves, peeled and finely chopped
2 teaspoons finely chopped fresh rosemary, plus a few needles
sea salt, black pepper
2 red-skinned eating apples, quartered, cored and thinly sliced lengthways

Preheat the oven to 180°C fan/200°C electric/gas 6. Toss the celeriac and carrot separately in large bowls with 3 tablespoons of olive oil (1½ tablespoons in each), the garlic, chopped rosemary, and some seasoning. Arrange the celeriac in a layer in a gratin or shallow ovenproof dish (about 20 x 30cm), with the carrot on top, cover tightly with foil and bake for 50 minutes until the vegetables are tender when pierced with a knife.

Scatter the apple over the surface, and a few rosemary needles, drizzle over another tablespoon of oil and return to the oven for 15 minutes, then pop under the grill to colour the top.
Carbohydrate 15.5g Protein 2.1g

Mixed mushroom fry-up

There is no rocket science to this recipe, if anything it is here as a reminder. I find if I am cooking something in season and there has been a gap of many months since the last time, I may have forgotten the way I felt was 'best', and need to look back at past notes and recipes.

Serves 4

4 tablespoons olive oil
2 shallots, peeled and finely chopped
1 garlic clove, peeled and finely chopped (optional)
450g mixture wild and cultivated mushrooms, picked over and sliced as necessary
sea salt, black pepper
a squeeze of lemon juice
2 heaped tablespoons finely chopped flat-leaf parsley

Fry the mushrooms in two goes. Heat half the oil in a large frying pan over a medium heat, add half the shallots and cook for a moment until they soften. Add half the garlic (if including) and half the mushrooms, turn up the heat and toss constantly until they are soft and starting to colour, seasoning them towards the end. If any liquid is given out in the process keep cooking until it evaporates. Remove the mushrooms to a bowl and cook the remainder likewise.

Return all the mushrooms to the pan, season with a squeeze of lemon juice and stir in the parsley.
Carbohydrate 2.5g Protein 2.4g

Tapas-style mushrooms

Eggs every which way come to mind as an accompaniment here, scrambled, poached or fried, in time for brunch, but there again an apéritif of a small glass of dry fino and it could be hard to choose.

Serves 6

3 tablespoons extra virgin olive oil
4 shallots, peeled, halved and sliced
10 thin slices of chorizo, cut into thin strips
500g chestnut and button mushrooms, trimmed, and halved if large
sea salt, black pepper
100ml Madeira or medium sherry
coarsely chopped coriander leaves

Heat 2 tablespoons of the olive oil in a large frying pan over a medium–high heat, add the shallots and chorizo and fry for 4–7 minutes until lightly golden, stirring occasionally. Add the mushrooms and another tablespoon of oil, season and fry for about 5 minutes longer, until the onions are a deep gold and the mushrooms lightly coloured.

Pour in the Madeira and simmer for a few minutes until the juices are really rich and dark. You can also cook these in advance and briefly reheat them.

Serve straightaway scattered with coriander.
Carbohydrate 2g Protein 3.4g

Root veg rösti

Any vegetable that is grated and then fried is going to make for deliciously delicate and crispy wisps, and these rösti which splay themselves in the pan are no exception. Ham? A tempting marriage, given the sweetness of the roots. Around Christmas can be the ideal time, when leftover shreds are going begging, but otherwise some pulled or shredded ham hock will play the part.

Serves 4

250g carrots, trimmed and peeled
250g swede, skin cut off
1 small onion, peeled
2 medium eggs
1 teaspoon grainy mustard
sea salt, black pepper
150g shredded or diced ham
   (optional)
groundnut or other vegetable oil for
   frying

Bring a large saucepan of salted water to the boil. Coarsely grate and combine the carrots, swede and onion – the quickest route here is a food processor using the coarse grating attachment, picking out any chunky slivers. Add the grated veg to the boiling water and blanch for 2 minutes, then drain into a sieve and press out as much liquid as possible using a potato masher. Transfer the grated veg to a large bowl and leave to cool to room temperature. You can prepare it to this point an hour or two in advance, in which case cover and set aside.

Whisk the eggs with the mustard and mix this into the vegetables, and season the mixture. Fold in the ham if wished. Heat a tablespoon of oil in a large, non-stick frying pan over a medium heat, and drop heaped tablespoons of the mixture into the pan, gently but firmly pressing each mound down with a spatula to form a patty about 1cm thick with ragged edges. You will probably be able to fit about 3 in the pan at a time. Fry for 2–3 minutes until the underside is golden and crispy, then carefully turn, using a spatula as they are quite delicate, and fry for a couple of minutes longer. Cook the remainder in the same fashion, adding more oil to the pan with each batch or as necessary. You should get 8–9 in all – they can be kept warm in a very low oven if wished.
Carbohydrate 9.6g Protein 4.3g

Flat-cap mushrooms baked with garlic, lemon and chilli

Simply a delicious way of cooking any kind of flat-cap mushrooms, using their gently concave cups to hold the juices given out as they bake, and mingle with the jazzy trio of garlic, chilli and lemon. Like any mushroom, the perfect aside to roast or grilled meat, or with bacon and fried eggs.

Serves 4

8 medium flat-cap mushrooms
4 garlic cloves, peeled and finely
    chopped
1 medium-hot red chilli, core and
    seeds removed and finely chopped
finely grated zest of 1 lemon, plus
    1 tablespoon of juice
3 tablespoons extra virgin olive oil
25g unsalted butter
sea salt, black pepper
2 tablespoons coarsely chopped
    flat-leaf parsley

Preheat the oven to 180°C fan/200°C electric/gas 6. Trim the ends of the mushroom stalks and arrange them in a roasting dish cup-side up. Divide the garlic, chilli and lemon zest between the cups. Drizzle over the olive oil, dot with the butter, season and bake for 25 minutes.

Remove from the oven, sprinkle the lemon juice over the mushrooms and scatter with parsley. Serve hot or warm.
Carbohydrate 1.6g Protein 2.7g

THE SALAD COUNTER

There is no point in pretending that bread and lettuce leaves have anything in common, but for as long as I can remember I have been using crisp green leaves to the same advantage that others do bread rolls. It started as a preference over crackers to go with cheese, I found a salty sliver of Comté or gooey river of Vacherin altogether more appealing when slipped on top of a small leaf, especially when there were walnuts to crack. Then it moved on to dipping slightly bitter leaves of Belgian chicory into taramasalata and guacamole or whatever I was grazing on, as opposed to a piece of pitta. While others would eat smoked salmon on a slice of buttered brown bread, my choice again was a leaf of lettuce.

So throughout this book, whenever I repeat my mantra of 'lettuce, lettuce, lettuce', please understand it is heartfelt, not something I am suggesting is a good idea simply in the name of reducing carbs. I would far sooner pair rich offerings with the clean austerity of salad than with the starchy dryness of a loaf.

So much of the way we eat is to do with conditioning and habit. Snacking on bread and toast is engrained into us from the earliest age, by busy mums for whom it represents the simplest home-cooked offering. If the bread is good and likewise what you put on it, surely that is better than a processed sausage-roll, or so the thinking goes. And then as we get older, probably as our first stab at independent living, most parents will suggest to their children making themselves some toast as an elementary exploration into cooking. Come college, if there is a communal kitchen, the likelihood is the provision will run to bread, butter, jam and the like, tea and coffee.

But it is possible to change the way you eat. In France, men of a certain age often sport what might politely be coined 'baguette belly'. The more traditional French, in areas where a two-hour lunchbreak is still the norm, will travel home at lunchtime, or perhaps go to a local restaurant where they will eat their main meal of the day. The two or three courses it entails are usually fairly healthy. Some salads to begin, then an entrée of meat and one or two veg, a sliver or two of cheese. But, it is quite usual for the diner to consume up to half a long baguette. Supper is likely to be a smaller meal, some *soupe* perhaps and a piece of fruit. But again the soup is consumed with another half baguette.

One of our neighbours in Normandy with a 'baguette belly' decided he wanted to lose it. So, he gave up his beloved loaf, which must have taken an iron will because I recall him refusing even to sit down to a meal if it was absent, and over the period of a year the weight simply dropped off him. That was the only change that he made in his diet. Frequently, I believe, it can be just one small change that is the difference between slowly putting on weight until you enter the rollercoaster ride of yo-yo dieting, and maintaining a healthy weight with which you are happy. If you habitually snack on bread, it could be that toning this down is all you need to do in order to stop gaining. So, lettuce leaf or bread?

Hot five dressings

GREEN GODDESS

This is much more than a dressing, voluptuously silken and creamy, like a mayonnaise you could slather it onto pretty much anything with assured results. It is likely to be a little more than you will need for the salad here, but as well as *crudités*, you could stir some cooked diced green vegetables and capers into it.

Serves 8

2 medium eggs
150ml extra virgin olive oil
2 tablespoons lemon juice
½ garlic clove, chopped
20g flat-leaf parsley
sea salt, black pepper

Bring a small saucepan of water to the boil and cook the eggs for 1 minute, then drain the pan, refill with cold water and leave them to cool for a couple of minutes. Scoop the insides of the eggs into a liquidiser, including the thin layer of cooked white lining the shell, and blend with all the remaining dressing ingredients to a creamy green emulsion. Cover and chill until required. The dressing will keep well for a couple of days.
Carbohydrate 0.3g Protein 1.7g

Serves 8

2 small heads Belgian chicory
60g watercress sprigs
60g pea shoots
2 avocados, quartered and stoned
1 punnet of mustard and cress, cut
50g pitted or stuffed green olives, halved
1 tablespoon snipped chives

SERVING SUGGESTION

Trim the base of the heads of the chicory, discard any damaged outer leaves, then cut in half lengthways and thinly slice, and halve again into shorter lengths. Combine these on a serving dish with the watercress and pea shoots. Peel the skin off the avocado quarters and cut into long thin strips.

Drizzle some of the dressing over the leaves, scatter over the avocado and drizzle over a little more, then dot with clumps of mustard and cress, scatter with olives and some chives.
Carbohydrate 1.3g Protein 3.4g

REAL FRENCH DRESSING

I love this particular dressing for its honest, flinty, down-to-earth profile. Sometimes we talk of vegetable oils as being neutral or tasteless, but they all have their own savour, however subtle. I prefer groundnut (or arachide) to sunflower oil, and I also find it tends to emulsify better, so unless you are avoiding peanuts this will give the best results.

Serves 6

1 rounded teaspoon Dijon mustard
sea salt, black pepper
3 tablespoons groundnut oil
1 teaspoon vinegar, (red wine or cider)

Whisk the mustard with a little seasoning in a medium bowl, scrunching the salt if it is flaky. Whisk in the oil a tablespoon at a time, until thick and mayonnaise-like. Stir in the vinegar and then about 2 teaspoons of water to thin the vinaigrette to the consistency of single cream.
Carbohydrate 0.3g Protein 0.1g

ANCHOVY AND LEMON
One of the best dressings for chicories, be it Belgian or the leafier types and endive.

Serves 4

finely grated zest of 1 lemon, plus
    2 tablespoons juice
6 salted anchovy fillets, finely
    chopped
1 teaspoon finely chopped
    medium-hot red chilli
sea salt
9 tablespoons extra virgin olive oil

Whisk together the lemon zest and juice, anchovies, chilli and a little salt in a medium bowl, then whisk in the oil.
Carbohydrate 0.2g Protein 1.6g

SERVING SUGGESTION
Chicory gives out lots of liquid once it's dressed, especially in the company of anchovies, so toss it as close to eating as possible.

Serves 4

8 heads (about 800g) of Belgian
    chicory, ideally red
a handful of coarsely chopped
    flat-leaf parsley

Trim the base of the heads of chicory, discard any damaged outer leaves, then cut in half lengthways and thinly slice into long thin strips. Transfer to a salad bowl, pour over the dressing and toss, then mix in some parsley.
Carbohydrate 8.3g Protein 3g

CAESAR

In a true Caesar salad the dressing is only half the story, with Parmesan sharing the stage. But actually it's a great dressing in its own right, and I frequently use it on its own with salads. Its tendency towards bitter/sharp makes it good for slightly sweeter salads, which could be as simple as the addition of some avocado or tomato. It's a good one when you want something with the luxurious quality of a mayonnaise, that is considerably easier to make.

Serves 8

2 medium eggs
½ garlic clove, chopped
2 tablespoons lemon juice
2 teaspoons Worcestershire sauce
150ml extra virgin olive oil
sea salt, black pepper

Bring a small saucepan of water to the boil and cook the eggs for 1 minute, then drain the pan, refill with cold water and leave them to cool for a couple of minutes. Scoop the insides of the eggs into a liquidiser, including the thin layer of cooked white lining the shell, and blend with all the remaining dressing ingredients to a pale and creamy emulsion. Cover and chill until required. The dressing will keep well for a couple of days.
Carbohydrate 0.4g Protein 1.6g

SERVING SUGGESTION

This is a basic Caesar salad, you can build it up in any way you wish, with slivers of avocado and chicken, crispy bacon, other leaves or finely sliced radishes.

Serves 4

4 Romaine lettuce hearts
70g freshly grated Parmesan

Separate out the lettuce leaves, discarding any outer leathery or blowsy dark green leaves (these can be saved for a soup or purée, or trimmed for slicing into another salad). Arrange the Romaine leaves on two large sharing plates or four dinner plates. Pour over some of the dressing, scatter over the Parmesan and serve straight away.
Carbohydrate 1.8g Protein 8.7g

SOUR CREAM AND MUSTARD

Another rich and voluptuous dressing that is mayonnaise-like in style. This makes for a generous quantity; I find it has many uses, but half this amount should do you for a family supper. A little sugar to taste is not a bad idea if dressing cabbage, for instance, or leaves that have a bitter edge.

Serves 6

225g sour cream
2 teaspoons Dijon mustard
a squeeze of lemon juice
sea salt, black pepper

Combine all the ingredients in a medium bowl, cover and chill until required. It will keep well for several days.
Carbohydrate 1.8g Protein 1.2g

Leafy ensembles

Almost any selection of salad leaves that you assemble is going to be streets ahead of a pre-pack: there is nothing to beat leaves that have been carefully picked over by hand and then washed in a sink of very cold water to crisp and restore their just-picked nascence.

My mother, I remember, always used to wrap the leaves in a tea towel and give it a good shake outside to dry them, which as far as I could tell seemed to involve transferring the water from your leaves to your clothes. A salad spinner is very much easier and assures perfectly dry leaves, without damaging them. It is one piece of kit worth investing in (see page 14); flimsy spinners or ones with pull strings make my mother's method seem skilled.

Layer **Little Gem heart leaves**, **lamb's lettuce** or **pea shoots**, and finally **mustard and cress** or **micro leaves**.

Combine **lamb's lettuce** with **baby ruby chard** or **baby spinach**, and **red or green mustard and cress**. Also lovely with cooked **asparagus spears**.

Combine sliced **Little Gem hearts** and quartered heads of **red chicory (endive)**, with **alfalfa sprouts**, **pea shoots**, and sliced **breakfast radishes**.

Combine thickly sliced **Romaine lettuce heart**, with **lamb's lettuce**, **watercress sprigs**, **mustard and cress**, and thinly sliced **spring onions**.

Combine small **watercress sprigs**, **pea shoots** or **lamb's lettuce**, inner leaves from a **round green lettuce** with peeled and very finely sliced **cucumber**, scattering over thinly sliced **spring onions**.

Big blowsy lettuces like **escarole** and **batavia**, or other **round green lettuces**, will star on their own. Throw in some crispy **lardons** and scatter with sliced **spring onions**.

Scatter a floppy **round green lettuce** with finely chopped **shallot** and snipped **chives**.

Combine **baby spinach** with thinly sliced **Belgian chicory (endive)**.

Mix up cresses – **rocket**, **watercress** and **mustard and cress** for a punchy peppery salad.

SALAD EXTRAS
raw or cooked beetroot
coarsely grated carrot
finely sliced radishes
finely sliced cucumber
finely shaved fennel
finely diced red onion
sliced button mushrooms
pomegranate seeds
slivers of apple
avocado
cooked green beans and mangetouts
capers
olives
lardons
quails' eggs

ABOVE LEFT TO RIGHT: *Real French Dressing (see page 194), Caesar (see page 196) and Anchovy and Lemon (see page 195)*

ABOVE LEFT TO RIGHT: *Green Goddess (see page 194) and Sour Cream and Mustard (see page 196)*

ICONIC SALADS

Sausage, egg and bacon salad

Full English breakfast in salad form and, like the *Salade Niçoise* on page 132, wholly sustaining, great for when you are ravenously hungry. But, despite its British sentiments, you need a sausage that is all meat, such as a Toulouse – cooked chorizo would also be good. Equally, explore locally produced sausages of the rusk-free genre. As more and more people eschew gluten these are becoming a firm fixture.

Serves 4

Salad:
3 eggs
100g French beans, stalk ends
    trimmed, halved
8 rashers rindless unsmoked streaky
    bacon
1 Romaine lettuce (or similar)
2 tomatoes, cut into wedges
3 cooked sausages, eg Toulouse,
    at room temperature, slit in half
    lengthways, then cut in half

Dressing:
½ teaspoon Dijon mustard
½ teaspoon wholegrain mustard
2 teaspoons red wine vinegar
sea salt, black pepper
3 tablespoons extra virgin olive oil
3 tablespoons groundnut oil

Bring a small saucepan of water to the boil and cook the eggs for 7 minutes, then drain the pan, refill with cold water and leave them to cool. Bring a second pan of salted water to the boil, add the beans and cook for 3–4 minutes until just tender. Drain into a sieve, refresh under the cold tap, and set aside.

At the same time heat the grill, and cook the bacon rashers on both sides until golden and crispy. Leave to cool, then cut in half. Discard any tough outer leaves from the lettuce and slice the remaining head into 2.5cm strips. Wash, dry and place in a large bowl. Add the beans, tomatoes and sausages to the bowl with the lettuce.

To make the dressing, whisk the mustards, vinegar and some seasoning in a bowl, add the oils and whisk until the dressing emulsifies into a thin cream. Toss the dressing with the salad ingredients in the bowl. Shell and halve the eggs and gently fold first the bacon and then the eggs into the salad.

Carbohydrate 4.5g Protein 23.4g

Asparagus Russian salad

The asparagus in this salad raises the bar, but you could simply double up on the French beans and sugar snaps. The essence here is the cocktail of different vegetables cloaked in the comfort of a creamy dressing, with the lively burst of capers and tarragon.

Serves 4

Salad:
400g celeriac, skin cut off and cut into 1cm dice
a bunch of asparagus (about 300g), trimmed
100g fine French beans, topped and tailed, and cut into 1cm dice
100g sugar snap peas, topped and tailed and cut into 1cm dice
2 tablespoons small capers, (eg nonpareille), rinsed, plus a few extra to serve
2 teaspoons finely chopped fresh tarragon, or 2 tablespoons chopped fresh chervil
2 spring onions, trimmed and finely sliced

Mayonnaise:
100g mayonnaise
100g sour cream
1 heaped teaspoon Dijon mustard
sea salt
cayenne pepper

Bring two medium saucepans of salted water to the boil. Add the celeriac to one and cook for 7–8 minutes or until just tender. Drain into a colander and set aside to cool.

In the meantime, cut off the asparagus tips and slice the remaining stalks into 1cm lengths. Add the French beans and asparagus to the second pan, and simmer for 3 minutes, adding the sugar snaps after 1 minute. Drain everything into a colander and refresh under the cold tap, then leave to cool completely.

To assemble the salad, blend the mayonnaise with the sour cream, mustard and a little salt in a large bowl. Setting aside the asparagus tips, add the remaining green vegetables to the bowl, along with the celeriac, capers, tarragon or chervil and spring onions. Gently stir to combine, then transfer these to a serving dish. Scatter over the asparagus tips and few more capers, and dust with a smidgeon of cayenne pepper. Cover and chill until required – unusually, this salad will keep well overnight.
Carbohydrate 7.5g Protein 5.6g

AKA potato salad

Celeriac stands in for potatoes? From our love of remoulade we know how good it can be in a salad. Playing the pretender, this stands in for a potato salad, with cold roast chicken or prawns.

Serves 6

Salad:
400g celeriac, skin cut off and cut into 1cm dice
150g cherry tomatoes, quartered
1 tablespoon small capers, (eg nonpareille), rinsed
4 tablespoons coarsely chopped flat-leaf parsley, plus extra to serve

Dressing:
100g sour cream
100g mayonnaise
1 teaspoon grainy mustard
sea salt
1 tablespoon finely chopped shallot

Bring a medium saucepan of salted water to the boil, add the celeriac and cook for 7–8 minutes or until just tender. Drain into a colander and set aside to cool.

To make the dressing, blend the sour cream, mayonnaise and mustard in a large bowl with a little salt. Stir in the shallot, then add the celeriac and gently toss. Reserving a few tomatoes, mix in the remainder with the capers and parsley. Transfer to a dish or bowl, scatter over the reserved tomatoes and a little more parsley. The salad can be made several hours in advance, in which case cover and chill until required, removing from the fridge 30 minutes in advance of eating.
Carbohydrate 3.5g Protein 1.9g

Guacamole

Dicing everything by hand takes longer, but the results are a tad more refined. But the speedy route of whizzing everything in a food processor is good for dipping and serving as a sauce.

Combine 100g quartered **cherry tomatoes**, one-eighth of a finely diced **red onion** and 1 teaspoon of finely diced **medium-hot red chilli** in a bowl, add 2 tablepoons of **lime** or **lemon juice**, 2 tablespoons of **extra virgin olive oil** and some **sea salt** and toss. Spoon in the flesh of 5 **avocados** cut into 1cm dice and gently toss, then mix in 2 tablespoons of coarsely chopped **coriander**. Try to make this within about 2 hours of serving, before the avocado discolours.
Carbohydrate 2.2g Protein 1.8g (Serves 8)

SPEEDY GUACAMOLE
Omitting the tomatoes, whizz the ingredients in a food processor, you can replace the chilli with **Tabasco**. You can embellish this by scattering with sliced **cherry tomatoes**, a drizzle of **olive oil** and some chopped **coriander**.

Frisée and lardons

A whole frisée lettuce is a pleasure to encounter, the blanched inner pale green fronds at the heart marry so well with salty lardons and a sharp mustardy vinaigrette. These lettuces can vary enormously in size, so if it's a huge blowsy affair, use enough leaves for 4 and reserve the remainder for another salad. Frisées keep well for several days wrapped in a plastic bag in the salad drawer of the fridge.

The best way to prepare a frisée lettuce is to hold it by the stalk and give it a radical trim around the edges, removing several inches of the dark green leaves, which are tough and too bitter to eat. Now cut out the stalk and discard the outside leaves. Separate and tear up the remaining pale green fronds and wash them in a sink of cold water. Shake or spin them dry.

Serves 4

Salad:
120g fine French beans, topped, tailed and halved
frisée leaves to serve 4
6 large cherry tomatoes, cut into wedges
175g unsmoked lardons, or diced rindless streaky bacon

Dressing:
1 tablespoon Dijon mustard
2 teaspoons red wine vinegar
sea salt
3 tablespoons groundnut oil

Bring a small saucepan of salted water to the boil, add the beans and simmer for 3–4 minutes to leave them firm to the bite. Drain, refresh them in cold water, then toss them into the leaves along with the tomatoes.

To make the dressing, whisk the mustard with the vinegar and some sea salt in a small bowl, then whisk in the oil.

Heat a dry frying pan over a medium–low heat and fry the lardons for about 8 minutes in the rendered fat, stirring occasionally, until golden. Drain on a double thickness of kitchen paper. These can be used while warm or at room temperature.

To serve, toss the salad with the dressing, then scatter over the lardons.
Carbohydrate 2.2g Protein 8.5g

LOW CARB PUDS

So, where do we stand on doughnuts? Out. Meringues? Out. Sticky toffee pudding? Off the scale, forget it. OK, a fruit salad? Actually, only in moderation. As a rule of thumb the sweeter it tastes, the more carbs it contains. At least give or take, because some fruits are better than others. If you do want to indulge, the ones to home in on are berries – raspberries, blackberries, strawberries are all great – and others – such as melon, kiwi and plums – are also pretty good, but then grapes and bananas, again to be avoided.

So the rules here are curious, and should you want to carb-count then it is worth consulting McCance and Widdowson's *The Composition of Foods* (see page 13) which is the best authority on the subject. Pedantic carb-counting is not generally a consideration in this book, the idea being that you can get away with eating as much as you want without worrying, but once we stray into sweet food all that changes.

Perhaps more poignantly, the guidelines regarding the constantly pedalled 'five-a-day' in relation to how much fruit we should eat are at best confusing, and worst absent. Or, as the nutritionist Dr Prechtl, who specialises in treating obesity, puts it, 'if you eat five portions of fruit a day you are going to put on weight.' She suggests aiming for no more than two portions a day, with the remaining three being made up of vegetables. Even then if you actively want to lose weight, simply cut fruit out altogether. Perhaps the best way to regard fruit, is as a vegetable with added sugar. The real importance within your five-a-day is to aim for a variety of colours, which should give you the best range of nutrients.

But back to puds, and those times when the call comes for something sweet, a birthday, a weekend treat or at the end of dinner. What follows are the ones I find the most useful. They are 'Lower carb', and more or less abide by the rules of plenty of protein, a little in the way of fruit, and easy on the fat. The essential thing is that there's chocolate cake, which tastes so decadently rich it is hard to believe just how clean-living it is. I'm not suggesting you live off it, but it's still wildly better than doughnuts, or sticky toffee pudding.

Very dark and moussey chocolate cake

This cake has all the credentials of a rich chocolate cake, it is indecently gooey with a heady hit of dark chocolate, and you only need the smallest sliver at the end of dinner to feel suitably spoilt. Broken down however, the 'smallest sliver' translates to something like two prunes, a little orange juice, a third of an egg, a fine shaving of butter and a couple of squares of cocoa-rich chocolate. In short, nothing to beat yourself up about.

The cake can also boast being gluten-free, and it's great for rounding off a special lunch or dinner with a big plate of fruit in attendance, such as one of the suggestions on page 210.

Makes 1 x 20cm cake
Serves 10

200g stoned prunes
200ml smooth orange juice
125g unsalted butter, diced, plus extra for the tin
200g dark chocolate (about 85% cocoa), broken into pieces
1 tablespoon dark rum (optional)
6 medium eggs, separated
cocoa for dusting

Place the prunes in a small saucepan with half the orange juice and simmer over a medium heat, stirring occasionally, until the fruit is sitting in a small amount of sticky syrup. Transfer the prunes and syrup to a food processor and reduce to a thick purée.

Preheat the oven to 160°C fan/180°C electric/gas 4 and butter a 20cm cake tin with sides 7cm deep and a removable base. Gently melt the butter and chocolate in a large mixing bowl set over a saucepan with a little simmering water in it. Whizz this with the prunes in the food processor (don't worry that initially it will turn claggy), then with the motor running, drizzle in the remaining orange juice, and the rum, if including, at which point the mixture should loosen and become creamy. Transfer it to a large bowl.

Whisk the yolks for a couple of minutes in a medium bowl using an electric whisk until very pale, moussey and doubled in volume. Fold these into the chocolate mixture in two goes. Now whisk the egg whites until stiff in a large bowl (using clean beaters), fold a third into the mixture to loosen it, and then the remainder in two goes. Pour the mixture into the prepared tin, smooth the surface and bake for 15 minutes until the cake appears slightly risen around the outside and the surface has set with a glossy sheen, it will remain wet in the centre.

Run a knife around the top edge and leave it to cool in the tin, then loosely cover and chill for several hours or overnight. Lightly dust with cocoa just before serving, then remove the collar. The cake is delicious either chilled or at room temperature, when it will be soft and mousse-like. It will keep for several days and freezes well.
Carbohydrate 13.9g Protein 6.5g

Strawberry and melon cocktail

A summery fruit platter, the loveliest of combinations that takes its inspiration from those kitsch retro cocktail bowls filled with melon balls, not something we tend to have time to prepare these days, or the kit to make them. But it's a good one to have in the fridge on a summer's day for dipping into, as well as eating after dinner.

Serves 4

¼ Galia or Cantaloupe melon, skin and seeds removed, cut into 8 thin segments
300g strawberries, hulled and halved unless small, or wild strawberries
300g seeded watermelon flesh, cut into 1–2cm dice

Place a couple of slivers of melon on each plate, and scatter over the strawberries and watermelon.
Carbohydrate 11.9g Protein 1.2g

Orange and passionfruit salad

A good winter fruit salad, which plays on the subtle differences between oranges and satsumas or clementines. The passionfruit seeds highlight their character. It's lovely for breakfast to kickstart your day as well as at the end of dinner.

Serves 6

200ml smooth orange juice
a squeeze of lemon juice
3 large oranges
4 satsumas or clementines
3 passionfruit, halved

Simmer the orange juice in a small saucepan until reduced by half, then pour into a bowl, add a squeeze of lemon juice and leave to cool.

Using a small sharp (ideally serrated) knife, cut a slice off the top and bottom of each orange, and cut the skin and pith off the sides, exposing the orange flesh. Slice across, 1cm thick, and remove any pips. Peel the satsumas or clementines, cut off and discard a thin slice on the top and bottom, and slice across 1cm thick. Arrange the fruit slices on a serving plate or in a shallow dish. Pour over the orange juice and spoon over the passionfruit seeds.
Carbohydrate 17g Protein 2.1g

Strawberry mousse

The absence of cream is the making of this mousse, it is as light as air, almost a foam. But the strawberries do need to be seasonally sweet and aromatic; out-of-season berries from countries that grow them solely for export will produce a suitably dull mousse.

Serves 4

2 gelatine leaves, cut into
    broad strips
200ml apple juice
200g strawberries, hulled
100g ricotta
½ teaspoon vanilla extract
2 medium organic egg whites
1 heaped teaspoon caster sugar
a few slivers of strawberry or wild
    strawberries, to serve

Place the gelatine in a medium-size bowl, cover with cold water and leave to soak for 5 minutes, then drain. At the same time simmer the apple juice until it reduces to a quarter of the volume (ie 50 ml). Pour this over the gelatine and stir to dissolve, then leave for about 5 minutes to cool a little.

Whizz the strawberries with the ricotta and vanilla in a liquidiser, and pass through a sieve into a medium-size bowl. Gradually stir in the gelatine solution. Whisk the whites until stiff in a medium-size bowl using an electric whisk, then sprinkle over the sugar and continue whisking for about 20 seconds until glossy. Fold this, half at a time, into the strawberry base. Divide between four 150ml ramekins or glasses, cover and chill for half a day or overnight. Serve with a few slivers of strawberry or wild strawberries on top.
Carbohydrate 10.7g Protein 6.8g

Blueberry and apple jelly

I love the lively profile of this jelly, as sweet as it is tart, and the blueberries and pomegranate seeds both provide their distinct charm. If it happened to be the season for elderflowers, you could simmer the juice with a couple of flowering heads and then strain it through a fine sieve, but otherwise an apple and elderflower juice will give it a lovely wine-like savour.

Serves 6

1.2 litres clear apple juice
4 gelatine leaves, cut into broad
    strips
300g blueberries
seeds from 1 pomegranate to serve
    (optional)

Bring the apple juice to the boil in a medium saucepan and reduce by half. In the meantime, put the gelatine strips in a medium bowl, cover with cold water and leave to soak for 5 minutes, then drain. Pour the apple juice over the gelatine and stir to dissolve, then leave to cool.

Pour the jelly solution into a serving bowl, ideally glass, and stir in the blueberries which will float. Cover and chill for half a day or overnight until set. Serve the jelly scattered with pomegranate seeds if wished. If you prefer, you can make the jelly in 6 individual glasses.
Carbohydrate 23.2g Protein 2g

Jelly mess

As refreshing as a long cooling drink at the end of dinner – a stack of easy fruit jellies that are crumbled before being layered with pomegranate seeds.

Serves 6

9 gelatine leaves, cut into
    broad strips
300ml apple juice
300ml red grape juice
300ml smooth orange juice
3 squeezes of lemon juice
seeds from 2 pomegranates

Divide the gelatine strips between three medium bowls, cover with cold water and leave to soak for 5 minutes, then drain them. Pour a couple of tablespoons of boiling water over each batch, and stir to dissolve, then very slowly whisk one juice into each bowl, then add a squeeze of lemon. Cover and chill overnight until set.

Run a fork through each jelly flavour to break it up into a soft, crumbly mass, or run a knife through it in a criss-cross pattern to dice it. Divide the apple one between six narrow 200ml glasses, spoon a third of the pomegranate seeds on top, then continue layering with jelly and pomegranate seeds, next using the red grape one, and lastly the orange one. These can be assembled well in advance, in which case cover and chill them.
Carbohydrate 16.2g Protein 4.8g

Crustless mango cheesecake

This cultural hotchpotch is halfway between a German cheesecake and a crustless Sicilian one, taking advantage of quark which is low in fat and high in protein. I would serve this with the berry sauce, or some raspberries and strawberries.

Makes 1 x 20cm cheesecake
Serves 10

Cheesecake:
100g unsalted butter, melted, plus extra for tin
200ml smooth orange juice, plus a little for the glaze
300g mango flesh
finely grated zest of 1 lemon
50g caster sugar
750g quark
3 large eggs, separated
a pinch of sea salt
1 teaspoon vanilla extract

Top:
1 gelatine leaf, cut into broad strips
4 passionfruit, halved

Preheat the oven to 160°C fan/180°C electric/gas 4 and butter a 20cm cake tin with sides 7cm deep and a removable base. Simmer the orange juice in a small saucepan until reduced to a quarter of the volume, ie 50ml.

Place the mango in a food processor with the orange juice, lemon zest and sugar and reduce to a smooth puree, then add the quark, egg yolks and salt and continue to whizz until smooth, and finally incorporate the melted butter and vanilla. Press this mixture through a sieve into a large bowl. Whisk the egg whites in another large bowl until stiff using an electric whisk, and fold into the cheesecake mixture in two goes. Transfer this to the prepared tin, smoothing the surface, and bake for 30 minutes until slightly risen and just set, it should still appear loose in the centre if you jig it from side to side.

Run a knife around the collar of the cheesecake, then return to the turned off oven for 10 minutes, propping the door open using a wooden spoon. Remove and leave to cool completely, setting the tin on a wire rack over a plate or a folded tea-towel, when some of the liquid will drain out of the cheesecake, which is completely normal with this type of curd. Don't worry if cracks appear in the centre as the passionfruit filling will cover them.

Place the gelatine in a measuring jug, cover with cold water and soak for 5 minutes, then drain. Pour over 3 tablespoons of boiling water and stir to dissolve. Stir the passionfruit pulp a tablespoon at a time into the gelatine solution, you should have about 150 ml, if not make it up with orange juice. Pour this over the top of the cheesecake within the crater-like rim, then loosely cover with foil and chill for another few hours or overnight. It is best eaten within a day or so.
Carbohydrate 15g Protein 14.2g

WITH A BERRY SAUCE
Whizz 200g hulled **strawberries** and 200g **raspberries** with 10g of **caster sugar** and a squeeze of **lemon juice**, and press through a sieve. Serve drizzled over the cheesecake.
Carbohydrate 18.2g Protein 14.6g

Index

Acknowledgements

I did at the outset, wonder if writing this book might not be seen as part of a cynical business plan. First you write a book about cake, then you write another about how to get rid of the weight. But, I do not know anyone who hasn't at some point in their life had to address a few extra pounds, be it after having a baby, or through the slow but steady expansion that comes with age. Understanding how our bodies work and what we can do to reduce our weight, with the minimum of effort, and in a way that is sustainable in the long-term can only be of benefit. I wish I had known at the age of 20 what I know today.

I am particularly indebted to Dr Alexander D. Miras MRCP, PhD, Clinical Lecturer in Metabolic Medicine at Imperial College, London, for his support throughout, and for sharing the results of years of trials and research into the treatment of weight loss. It has turned the book into a collaboration – a meeting of science with a personal passion for cooking and eating well. I am also indebted to Dr Christina Prechtl who works alongside Dr Miras, for approving the copy and sharing her recommendations and guidelines for how to eat.

It was a particular pleasure to have Kyle Cathie in person as Project Editor, ably assisted by Laura Foster. And thanks to the many people at Kyle Books who have also beavered away – Julia Barder as Sales and Marketing Director, Nic Jones and David Hearn in Production. Also to Stephanie Evans for copy editing the book, and to Jane Bamforth for proofreading it. While Wendy Doyle took on the task of analysing the nutritional value of all the recipes.

Dan Jones has done a wonderful job of capturing the home-cooked yummy spirit of the dishes, beautifully presented and prepared by the food stylist Annie Rigg, with Wei Tang chosing the tableware and backgrounds. It seems doubly spoiling to also have Sam Wilson's gorgeous line drawings, that are so timeless in the depiction of how we live and eat. Bringing it all together visually, huge thanks to Caroline Clark for her design of the book.

And lastly I am ever grateful to my agent Lizzy Kremer at David Higham for all her support. And to those immediate members of my family, Jonnie, Rothko and Louis who have been starved of potatoes and pasta for the duration, but, have continued to use this way of eating to their own advantage.

First published in Great Britain in 2014 by Kyle Books
an imprint of Kyle Cathie Ltd.
67–69 Whitfield Street
London, W1T 4HF
general.enquiries@kylebooks.com
www.kylebooks.com

10 9 8 7 6 5 4 3 2 1

ISBN: 978-0-85783-182-8

Project Editor: Kyle Cathie
Editorial Assistant: Laura Foster
Copy Editor: Stephanie Evans
Proofreader: Jane Bamforth
Designer: Caroline Clark
Photographer: Dan Jones
Illustrator: Sam Wilson
Nutritionist: Wendy Doyle
Food Stylist: Annie Rigg
Prop Stylist: Wei Tang
Production: Nic Jones and David Hearn

A Cataloguing In Publication record for this title is available from the
British Library.

Colour reproduction by ALTA London.
Printed and bound in China by C&C Offset Printing Company Ltd.